ARCHITECTURAL DESIGN

GUEST-EDITED BY
RIVKA OXMAN AND
ROBERT OXMAN

THE NEW STRUCTURALISM
DESIGN, ENGINEERING AND ARCHITECTURAL TECHNOLOGIES

04|2010

ARCHITECTURAL DESIGN
VOL 80, NO 4
JULY/AUGUST 2010
ISSN 0003-8504

PROFILE NO 206
ISBN 978-0470-742273

WILEY
wiley.com

ARCHITECTURAL DESIGN

GUEST-EDITED BY
RIVKA OXMAN AND
ROBERT OXMAN

THE NEW STRUCTURALISM
DESIGN, ENGINEERING AND ARCHITECTURAL TECHNOLOGIES

EDITORIAL BOARD
Will Alsop
Denise Bratton
Paul Brislin
Mark Burry
André Chaszar
Nigel Coates
Peter Cook
Teddy Cruz
Max Fordham
Massimiliano Fuksas
Edwin Heathcote
Michael Hensel
Anthony Hunt
Charles Jencks
Bob Maxwell
Jayne Merkel
Mark Robbins
Deborah Saunt
Leon van Schaik
Patrik Schumacher
Neil Spiller
Michael Weinstock
Ken Yeang
Alejandro Zaera-Polo

The renowned proponent of ultra–lightweight structures charts how his consultancy has developed a far–reaching approach to practice.

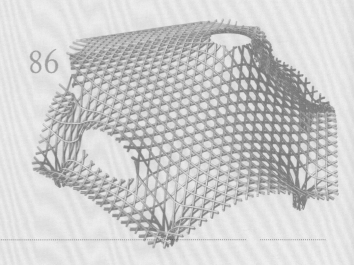

86

64

ARCHITECTURAL DESIGN
JULY/AUGUST 2010
PROFILE NO 206

Editorial Offices
John Wiley & Sons
25 John Street
London
WC1 N2BS

T: +44 (0)20 8326 3800

Editor
Helen Castle

Freelance Managing Editor
Caroline Ellerby

Production Editor
Elizabeth Gongde

Design and Prepress
Artmedia, London

Art Direction and Design
CHK Design:
Christian Küsters
Hannah Dumphy

Printed in Italy by Conti Tipocolor

Sponsorship/advertising
Faith Pidduck/Wayne Frost
T: +44 (0)1243 770254
E: fpidduck@wiley.co.uk

All Rights Reserved. No part of this publication may be reproduced, stored in a retrieval system or transmitted in any form or by any means, electronic, mechanical, photocopying, recording, scanning or otherwise, except under the terms of the Copyright, Designs and Patents Act 1988 or under the terms of a licence issued by the Copyright Licensing Agency Ltd, 90 Tottenham Court Road, London W1T 4LP, UK, without the permission in writing of the Publisher.

Subscribe to AD

AD is published bimonthly and is available to purchase on both a subscription basis and as individual volumes at the following prices.

Prices
Individual copies: £22.99/$45.00
Mailing fees may apply

Annual Subscription Rates
Student: UK£70/US$110 print only
Individual: UK £110/US$170 print only
Institutional: UK£180/US$335
print or online
Institutional: UK£198/US$369
combined print and online

Subscription Offices UK
John Wiley & Sons Ltd
Journals Administration Department
1 Oldlands Way, Bognor Regis
West Sussex, PO22 9SA
T: +44 (0)1243 843272
F: +44 (0)1243 843232
E: cs-journals@wiley.co.uk

[ISSN: 0003-8504]

Prices are for six issues and include postage and handling charges. Periodicals postage paid at Jamaica, NY 11431. Air freight and mailing in the USA by Publications Expediting Services Inc, 200 Meacham Avenue, Elmont, NY 11003.
Individual rate subscriptions must be paid by personal cheque or credit card. Individual rate subscriptions may not be resold or used as library copies.

All prices are subject to change without notice.

Postmaster
Send address changes to Publications Expediting Services Inc, 200 Meacham Avenue, Elmont, NY 11003

Rights and Permissions
Requests to the Publisher should be addressed to:
Permissions Department
John Wiley & Sons Ltd
The Atrium
Southern Gate
Chichester
West Sussex PO19 8SQ
England

F: +44 (0)1243 770620
E: permreq@wiley.co.uk

Front cover: Gramazio & Kohler (Architecture and Digital Fabrication, ETH Zurich), The Sequential Wall, Zurich, 2008. Image © Gramazio & Kohler, ETH Zurich
Inide front cover: Concept by CHK Design

The New Structuralism announces a new order in design and construction. With the onset of digital technologies, existing parameters have shifted. The old order of standardised design and its established processes no longer hold sway; contemporary architectural design can now be characterised by irregularity, and an appetite for producing customised non-standard, complex, curvilinear forms. The shift in design and production technologies requires a seamless design approach that fully acknowledges the interdependence of design and fabrication.

In this issue of △, Rivka Oxman and Robert Oxman are eloquently calling for a new model of architectural production in which architects and engineers work together in a higher level of collaboration. The structural engineer is no longer the fixer brought in during the late design stage to make a design work, but integral to the earliest generative stages. Design is no longer wholly dictated by form with structure following behind; structure becomes integral to form-finding. This message provides a refrain across the issue, and is most clearly articulated by Hanif Kara of Adams Kara Taylor (AKT), who calls for early input for engineers at conceptualisation stage. Dominik Holzer also describes the Optioneering research project undertaken between the Spatial Information Research Lab (SIAL) at the Royal Melbourne Institute of Technology (RMIT) and engineering firm Arup to explicitly investigate the capability of new forms of collaboration between architects and engineers. In her article, Neri Oxman takes the paradigm a step further and advocates the inversion of form–structure–material, placing material squarely first in the design sequence and making it the driver of structure and then design.

The Oxmans' carefully curated publication is a manifesto as much as an investigation into the current state of play. Architects have choices as to where to focus their energies and resources, and the emphasis that they want to place on specific aspects of their work – whether it be cultural or technical – especially in a constantly shifting economic and technological landscape. Counterpoint, a new series in △, commissioned independently by the editor, provides the opportunity to test the main thrust of the guest-edited issue. In the first Counterpoint, Neil Spiller counters the argument of the issue by questioning the hegemony of the dominant focus on new technologies and complex form-finding in architectural culture. Is this emphasis on the technical closing the door on human expression? △

Text © 2010 John Wiley & Sons Ltd. Image © Steve Gorton

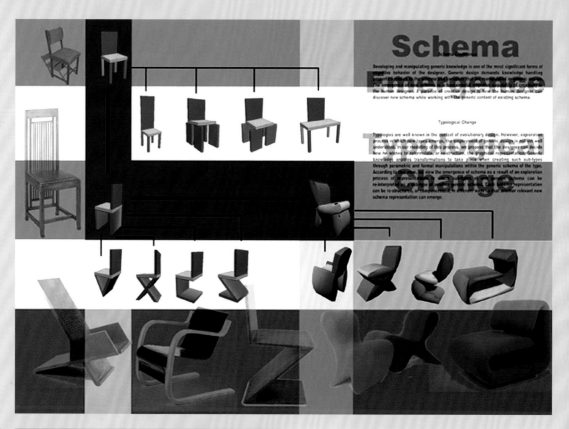

Schema

Developing and manipulating generic knowledge is one of the most significant forms of cognitive behavior of the designer. Generic design demands knowledge handling

Emergence

...the human designer. A paradox of creative design is how the human designer can discover new schema while working with the generic content of existing schema.

Typological Change

Typologies are well known in the context of evolutionary design. However, exploration process in which new types emerge, the employment of generic design is not well understood in our modeling of this process, we propose that the designer can discover new schema while working, or even create. The proposal represents a knowledge enables transformations to take place when creating such sub-types through parametric and formal manipulations within the generic schema of the type.

Change

According to this view the emergence of schema as a result of an exploration process of re-interpretation. Such schema can be re-structured, or changed, such that another relevant new schema representation can emerge.

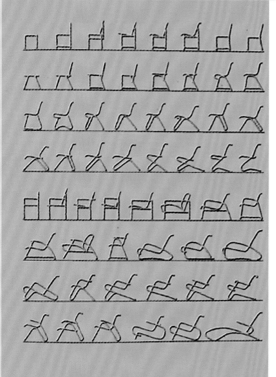

CDM
Cognative Design Media

Schema emergence as a paradox of generic design

how does design emergence differ from design evolution

Developing and manipulating generic knowledge is one of the most significant forms of cognitive behavior of the designer. Generic design demands knowledge handling properties related to the schema and variables which are manipulated in generic design. The emergence of new schema is a fundamental cognitive capability of creativity; in the human designer. A paradox of creative design is how the human designer can discover new schema while working with the generic content of existing schema (Dahmann, 1930) illustrated how a transformation process can occur in which specific prototypes of chairs can be transformed to other profiles. This and other works raise an interesting question how can specific typological knowledge contribute to the emergence of new types in creative thinking? Schema emergence thus appears to be a unique and highly significant form of emergence in the research literature. Our research attempts to cognitively model this class of emergence

Design system which supports schema emergence a computational approach.

what do we mean by emergence in computational terms?

In our approach, the computational environment behaves as a graphical interactive design medium which is supportive of the cognitive capabilities of the designer. Schema emergence is supported by providing an interactive interface which assists in the construction of new structures which can be derived from existing ones. The representational system operates through the maintenance of generic schema and topological knowledge while enabling modifications within the type. The topological generics act within the background while the designer interacts with the representation dynamically to achieve transformations. Once the limits of a typological schema have been reached to the designer he is free to transform the topological schema and then explore variations within the new typological framework.

Schema
Emergence

Professor Joseph Eidelman, Silos in Kiryat Gat, Israel, c 1972
above left: Rivka Oxman's father, the late Professor Eidelman, was one of Israel's pioneer structural engineers.

Rivka Oxman, Daniel Brainin, Hezi Golan and Eyal Nir, Schema Emergence Research Programme, Technion IIT, Israel, 1999–2001
above right: Models of schema emergence in creative design.

ABOUT THE GUEST-EDITORS
RIVKA OXMAN AND
ROBERT OXMAN

In the development of the field of design studies, one of the important areas of emerging knowledge has been the evolution of research, theories and experimental models related to processes of design. Rivka Oxman was one of the first researchers to explore the relationship between design thinking and computational models of design. For several decades she has been among the core body of international design researchers. In recognition of her contributions through research and publication to the understanding of architectural knowledge in models of design thinking and the role of knowledge in design education, she has been appointed a Fellow of the Design Research Society.

In recent years her work has attempted to reorient design thinking research to experimental models of digital design thinking. She has formulated novel information models of digital design such as generative and performance-based design. In defining and formulating these models in her research and writings, she has explored experimental pedagogy in architectural education as a medium to promote research-oriented design. Since 2006 she has been leading an experimental digital design studio at the Technion Israel Institute of Technology. She is an architect, researcher, author and educator. For the past four years she has been the Vice Dean of the Faculty of Architecture and Town Planning at the Technion. A prominent member of the international research community in design, she is also Associate Editor of *Design Studies* and a member of the editorial board of leading international journals. Current interests are the exploration of adaptive generative mechanisms of architectural and structural morphology and their ability to be responsive to changing environmental conditions.

The merging of theory and praxis in architecture and design has become an important influence upon current design. New vectors of theoretical activity, particularly in recent decades, have come to play an important role in emerging design practices. Robert Oxman is an architect, educator, writer and researcher in the field of architectural and design histories and theories. He was educated at Harvard College and the Harvard Graduate School of Design where he studied with Josep Lluís Sert and Fumihiko Maki. He is Professor and Dean Emeritus at the Technion and is currently Professor of Architectural and Design History and Theories at Shenkar College of Engineering and Design in Tel Aviv. At Shenkar, he is Dean of Graduate Studies and engaged in developing a unique programme of graduate education which integrates design, technology and industry.

Oxman has held the chairs of Design Methods and CAAD at the Technical University Eindhoven in the Netherlands. His work in architectural and design history and theories since 1945 has been published internationally. He is currently involved in researching and writing in three fields. The first, on design concepts, involves the evolution of architectural and design theories and practices after Modernism. This work also addresses the emergence of architectural and design research during this period. The second, undertaken in collaboration with Rivka Oxman, is the definition of the impact of digital design upon emerging theories and design practices. Currently entitled *The Digital in Design: Theory and Design in the Digital Age*, it is scheduled for publication by Taylor & Francis in 2011. The third area, involving architectural and design knowledge, relates to the role of knowledge in design, education and research, and particularly the significance of universal knowledge in a digital age. ⌂

Text © 2010 John Wiley & Sons Ltd. Images: p 6(l), 7 © Oxman and Oxman; p 7(r) © Rivka Oxman, Daniel Brainin, Hezi Golan, Eyal Nir

SPOTLIGHT

**Grimshaw Architects
with Buro Happold**

Milan E3 Exhibition Centre, Milan, 2006
The envelope of the centre was to be
formed out of parallel zinc-clad strips,
which, using only a minimum number of
radii, were to form openings and strips.

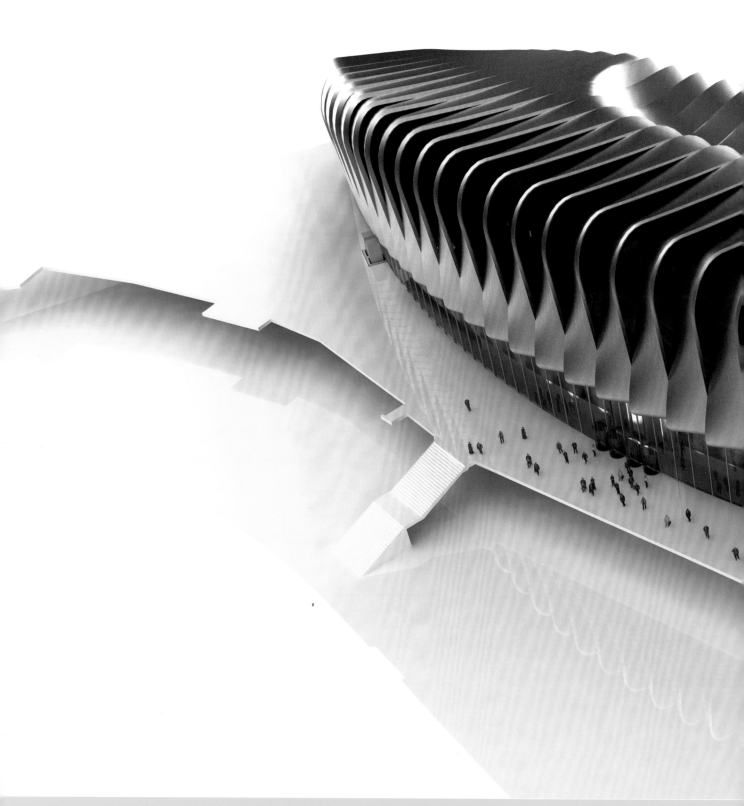

Earlier emphasis on structure and engineering with the High-Tech movement in the 1970s and 1980s led to an enthusiasm for showing the structure and a revival in enthusiasm for the pioneering engineers of the Victorian era. *The New Structuralism* embraces a wide range of formal approaches and materials, with varying degrees of complexity. All the projects share a non-standard approach to design in which elements are customised.

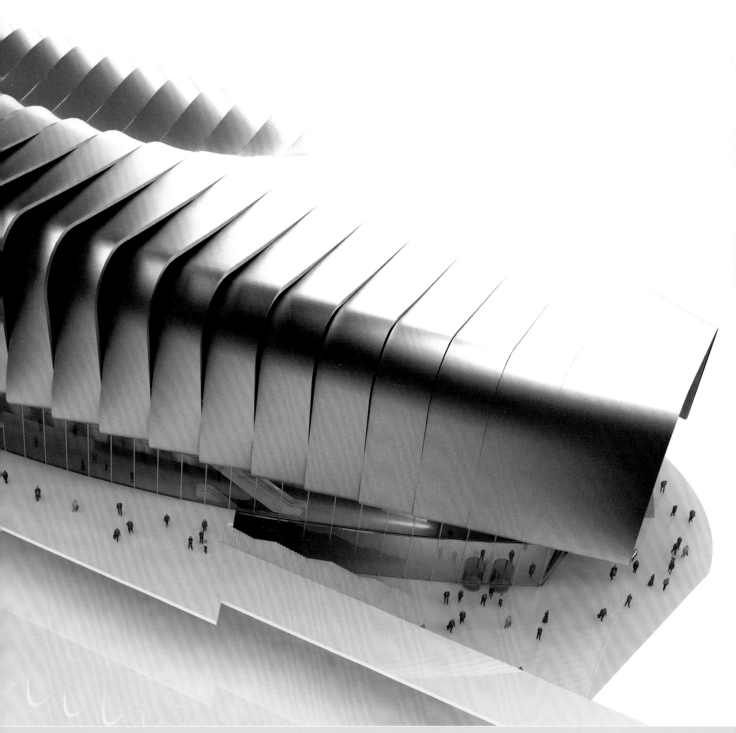

↑ **Heinz Isler**

↓ **Barkow Leibinger**

Heinz Isler with Copeland Associates and Haus + Herd, Tennis halls, Norfolk Health & Racquets Club, Norwich, UK, 1987
The tennis halls were designed by the experimental designer of free-form shell structures, Heinz Isler (1926–2009). A pioneer of free-form structures, he worked from handmade prototypes.

Light Structure, Hans Peter Jochum Gallery, Berlin, 2009
This laser-cut and scripted multicoloured Plexiglas tube lighting installation is the product of Barkow Leibinger's research and experimentation with cutting three-dimensional tube profiles.

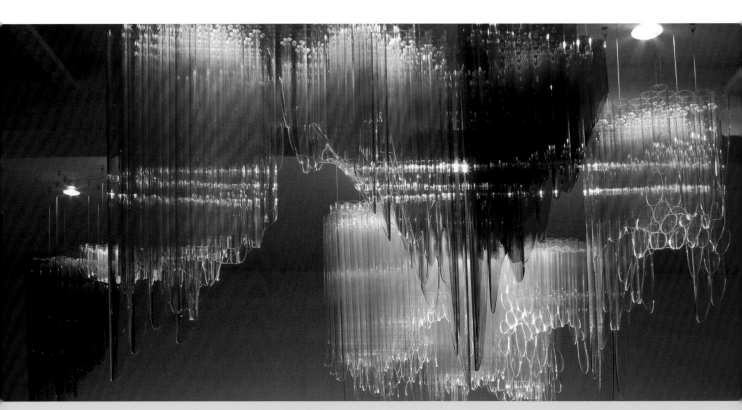

↑ **Neri Oxman**

Beast: Prototype for a Chaise Longue, Museum of Science, Boston, Massachusetts, 2009.
The chaise embodies Oxman's material approach, taking its lead from biological models. Like forms found in natural systems, it adapts its thickness, pattern, density, stiffness, flexibility and translucency to load, curvature and skin-pressured areas.

↓ **Gramazio & Kohler (Architecture and Digital Fabrication, ETH Zurich)**

West Fest Pavilion, Zurich, 2009
The pavilion is constructed out of standard wooden battens that are individually and precisely cut using robotic fabrication. The battens are stacked up to form columns that transform into a roof.

← **Reiser + Umemoto
with Ysrael A Seinuk**

0-14 Tower, Dubai, 2010
Playing with the notion of
structure, the architects
have given the exterior
surface a perforated bone-
like treatment.

↓ **Mutsuro Sasaki
and Arata Isozaki**

**Train station competition
scheme, Florence, 2002**
The rectilinear station is
enlivened by a seemingly
organic, free form – not unlike
a gnarled branch of a tree –
that simultaneously provides
structure and dynamism.

Text © 2010 John Wiley & Sons Ltd. Images: pp
8–9 © Grimshaw; p 10(t) © John Chilton; p 10(b)
© Corinne Rose; p 11(t) © Neri Oxman, Architect
and Designer; p 11(b) © Roman Keller; p 12 ©
Imre Solt; p 13 © Arata Isozaki & Associates

INTRODUCTION
*By Rivka Oxman
and Robert Oxman*

THE NEW STRUCTURALISM
DESIGN, ENGINEERING AND ARCHITECTURAL TECHNOLOGIES

Architecture is in the process of a revolutionary transformation. There is now momentum for a revitalised involvement with sources in material practice and technologies. This cultural evolution is pre-eminently expressed in the expanded collaborative relationships that have developed in the past decade between architects and structural engineers, relationships which have been responsible for the production, worldwide, of a series of iconic buildings. The rise and technological empowerment of these methods can be seen as a historic development in the evolution of architectural engineering. If engineering is frequently interpreted as the giving of precedence to material content, then the design engineer, in his prioritising of materialisation, is the pilot figure of this cultural shift which we have termed the 'new structuralism'.

Architectural engineering has traditionally been characterised by the sequential development of 'form, structure and material'. A formal concept is first conceived by the architect and subsequently structured and materialised in collaboration with the engineer. If there is a historical point of departure for the evolution of a new structuralism, Peter Rice, in *An Engineer Imagines*, locates it in the relationship which developed between Jørn Utzon, Ove Arup and Jack Zunz in the structuring and materialisation of the Sydney Opera House (1957–73).[1] In the final solution the problem of the geometry of the covering tiles influenced the design of the rib structure and the overall form of the roof. This effectively reversed the traditional process to become 'material, structure, form'.

Bernhard Franken and Bollinger + Grohmann, *Take-Off* sculpture, Munich Airport, 2003
The lamella structure of this work for BMW is an example of the relationship between design, fabrication technologies and principles, and the resultant creation of new materialities.

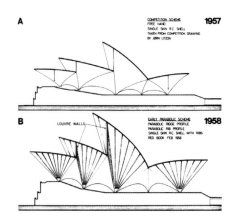
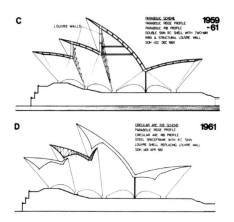
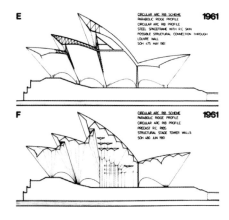

Jørn Utzon, Architect, Arup, Structural
Engineers, Sydney Opera House,
Sydney Australia, 1957–73
top: Development of the structure and
geometry of the shells for the Sydney
Opera House (Sir Jack Zunz, Arup).
Composite drawing from Peter Rice, *An
Engineer Imagines* (p 61), illustrating
the evolution of a material structure
in conformance with the geometric
fabrication constraints of the ceramic
covering tiles.

Werner Sobek,
Structuring Materiality,
'Nautilus' exhibition,
Dusseldorf, 2002
above: The placing of
a flexible skin over the
structure from which
the air volume has
been extracted creates
a 'new materiality'.

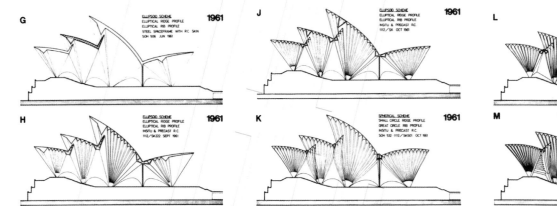

The role of material and structure in design expression occurred again, famously, in the hands of Edmund Happold and Peter Rice, with the cast-steel solution of the *gerberettes* of the main facade of the Centre Pompidou, Paris (1971–77). The thread of an emerging material practice in the collaborative work of architects and engineers has continued in a sequence of canonic works including those of Frei Otto, Edmund Happold, Jörg Schlaich and Mamoro Kawaguchi, and more recently in the collaborations of, among others, Cecil Balmond with Toyo Ito, Matsuro Sasaki with Toyo Ito, and Buro Happold with Shigeru Ban.

The Anatomy of Design Engineering

Over the last decade, 'design engineering'[2] has developed as a highly interactive medium for collaboration between architects and structural engineers. The approach has developed new models for the design of structures of geometric complexity that challenge orthodox methods of structural engineering. As a result, a series of processes have evolved which define a new relationship between the formal models of the architect and the materialising processes of the engineer.

The traditional designation of the interaction between the architect and engineer has frequently been one of post-rationalisation. Transcending that relationship, a new generation of structural engineers[3] has taken up a range of contemporary challenges such as dealing with the emerging professional responsibilities of incorporating new architectural technologies within the process of design. No longer *a posteriori*, the design engineer is now up-front at the earliest generative stage, bringing to the fore the design content of materialisation and fabrication technologies. It is characteristic of the cutting edge of contemporary engineering that the process has developed new media that mitigate between the optimisation of structural designs and the enhancement of the architectural concepts. If the ability to accommodate material considerations early in the design process is added to this emerging dynamic, it appears to be developing as an almost perfect model of design collaboration and is ultimately relevant to all classes of architectural practice.

Design Engineering as Paradigm

Contemporary design engineering is of very recent origin. Cecil Balmond has a unique position in establishing the profile, roles, design ambitions and research practices of the design engineer. In a three-decade career at Arup, his work, such as the long-term collaborations with Rem Koolhaas and involvement in enlightened projects such as the Serpentine pavilions, London, and particularly that with Toyo Ito in 2002, have spearheaded innovative form-finding. His publications and exhibitions have been of important cultural significance to architects and other disciplines, as well as to engineers.[4] The formation of the Advanced Geometry Unit (AGU) at Arup in 2000 was among the first of such interdisciplinary research groups in architectural and engineering offices, and Balmond's teaching in the architectural departments of Yale and Penn universities is characteristic of the significance of design engineering as a subject of interdisciplinary importance in defining the new knowledge base of architectural education. In his ability to deal with non-linear complexity, Balmond is also a proponent of the importance of the designer engineer's knowledge of mathematics and the geometric principles of structuring and patterning as part of a new design knowledge portfolio. Among other distinctions, he has reformulated design knowledge to include the mathematical and natural principles of 'structuring'.

This issue of *AD* introduces those aspects of the design engineering process that may have relevance for architectural design viewed as a material practice. The new structuralism integrates structuring, digital tectonics, materialisation, production and the research that makes this integration possible.

From Structure to Structuring

Structuring is the process whereby the logic of a unique parts-to-whole relationship develops between the elements of architecture. Historically, it is derivative of theory which provides a cultural designation of tectonics. Beyond the theoretical content, the new structuring provides the mathematical/geometric, syntactic and formal logic which is necessary for digital tectonics. Farshid Moussavi and Daniel Lopez-Perez state that: 'Tessellation moves architectural experiments away from mechanistic notions of systems which are used as tools for reproduction of forms, to machinic notions of systems that determine how diverse parts of an architectural problem interrelate to multiply each other and produce organizations of higher degree of complexity.'[5]

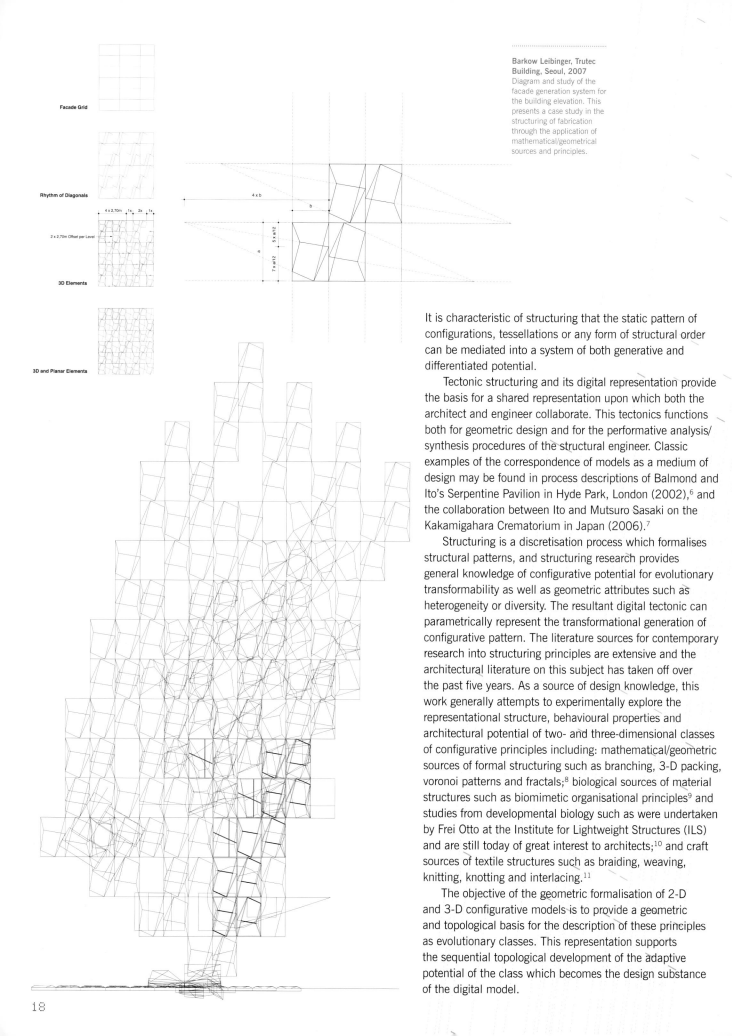

Facade Grid

Rhythm of Diagonals

4 x 2,70m   1x   2x   1x

2 x 2,70m Offset per Level

3D Elements

3D and Planar Elements

4 x b

b

a   5 x a/12

7 x a/12

Barkow Leibinger, Trutec
Building, Seoul, 2007
Diagram and study of the
facade generation system for
the building elevation. This
presents a case study in the
structuring of fabrication
through the application of
mathematical/geometrical
sources and principles.

It is characteristic of structuring that the static pattern of configurations, tessellations or any form of structural order can be mediated into a system of both generative and differentiated potential.

Tectonic structuring and its digital representation provide the basis for a shared representation upon which both the architect and engineer collaborate. This tectonics functions both for geometric design and for the performative analysis/synthesis procedures of the structural engineer. Classic examples of the correspondence of models as a medium of design may be found in process descriptions of Balmond and Ito's Serpentine Pavilion in Hyde Park, London (2002),[6] and the collaboration between Ito and Mutsuro Sasaki on the Kakamigahara Crematorium in Japan (2006).[7]

Structuring is a discretisation process which formalises structural patterns, and structuring research provides general knowledge of configurative potential for evolutionary transformability as well as geometric attributes such as heterogeneity or diversity. The resultant digital tectonic can parametrically represent the transformational generation of configurative pattern. The literature sources for contemporary research into structuring principles are extensive and the architectural literature on this subject has taken off over the past five years. As a source of design knowledge, this work generally attempts to experimentally explore the representational structure, behavioural properties and architectural potential of two- and three-dimensional classes of configurative principles including: mathematical/geometric sources of formal structuring such as branching, 3-D packing, voronoi patterns and fractals;[8] biological sources of material structures such as biomimetic organisational principles[9] and studies from developmental biology such as were undertaken by Frei Otto at the Institute for Lightweight Structures (ILS) and are still today of great interest to architects;[10] and craft sources of textile structures such as braiding, weaving, knitting, knotting and interlacing.[11]

The objective of the geometric formalisation of 2-D and 3-D configurative models is to provide a geometric and topological basis for the description of these principles as evolutionary classes. This representation supports the sequential topological development of the adaptive potential of the class which becomes the design substance of the digital model.

Judith Reitz and Daniel Baerlecken, Interlacing Structures Research Program, RWTH, Aachen, 2009
The research explores craft/ vernacular structuring principles such as knots, knitting and weaving within the general class of interlacing structures. It extrapolates these principles as tectonic systems and illustrates digital applications. This is characteristic of much contemporary design research in the field of digital structural morphologies.

The objective of the geometric formalisation of 2-D and 3-D configurative models is to provide a geometric and topological basis for the description of these principles as evolutionary classes.

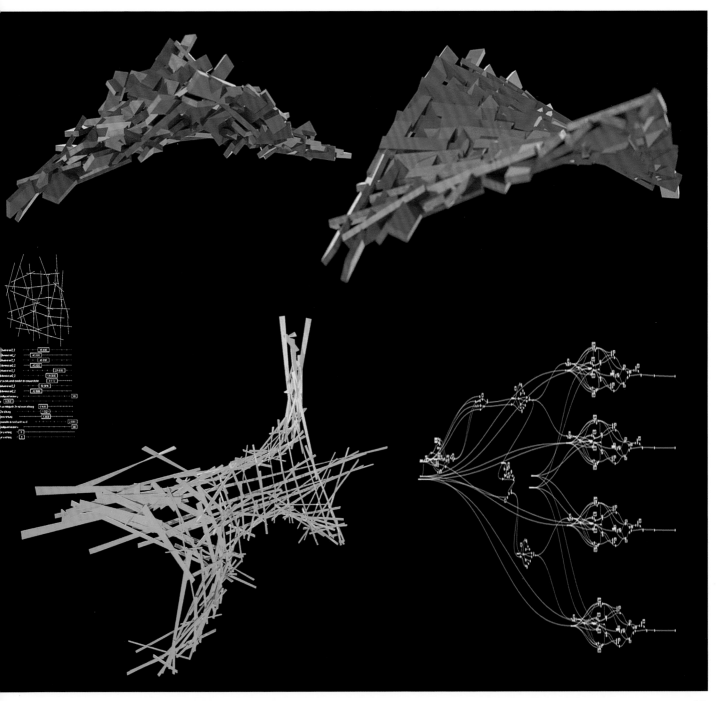

Future Systems and Adams Kara
Taylor (AKT), Strand Link Bridge, Land
Securities Headquarters, London, 2005
below: Digital tectonics and parametric
structural topologies are applied in
these studies by AKT for structuring and
fabrication proposals for materialising the
architectural concept.

Hanif Kara (AKT) and the Parametric Applied Research
Team (P.ART) with the AA School of Architecture and
Istanbul Technical University Faculty of Architecture,
Fibrous Concrete Workshop, Istanbul, 2007
opposite top right: Within the workshop, these sketches
are a case study in the relationship between parametric
tectonics and material/fabrication design. 'From Parametric
Tectonics to Material Design' has become a cornerstone of
digital pedagogical content in the New Structuralism.

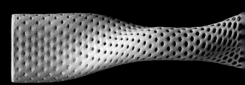

Digital Tectonics

Digital tectonics is the coincidence between geometric representations of structuring and the program that modulates them.[12] Some of the design and research processes associated with structuring are supported by such programs. Using digital tectonics, structural topologies can be modulated through encoding as parametric topologies.

Scripting is a medium for the generation of formal patterns and formal three-dimensional procedures in textile and craft structures.[13] Scripting programs are the design media of structuring. In digital tectonics scripting is used to produce geometric representations within the topology of the pattern or structure. Digital crafting is the ability to produce code that operates on the basis of such tectonic design models.

Associative geometry may support a design approach in which a geometrically, or tectonically, defined series of dependency relationships is the basis for a generative, evolutionary design process. Geometric variants of a class of structures can be generated parametrically by varying the values of its components; for example, the folds of a folded plate, or the grid cells of a mesh structure. Parametric software such as Bentley Systems' Generative Components or McNeel's Grasshopper for Rhino are media for the generative and iterative design of structuring that can produce the geometric representation of topological evolution. In recent years the Smart Geometry Group has done much to promote these innovative design techniques through its international conferences and teaching workshops.

Digital morphogenesis is the derivation of design solutions through generative and performative processes. It is a process of digital form-finding that has recently been employed in engineering practice by Mutsuro Sasaki[14] and discussed in the writings of the Emergence and Design Group.[15] Perhaps the highest level of performance-based design is the exploitation of performance data as the driver of the evolutionary design process. Digital morphogenesis will eventually achieve 'analysis driving generation/evolution'.

Structuring Materiality

As architecture begins to deal with fabrication as well as with construction, the architect/structural engineering team is poised to resume control of the central role of integrating architecture and its material technologies. The idea of material structures integrates the concepts of structuring, the behaviour of materials, and digital tectonics (see Yves Weinand and Markus Hudert's article on pp 102–7 of this issue). The study of material structures and their role in design and digital design has become a seminal subject of professional as well as academic concern. The research and understanding of the function of material in design, the ability to design with material, and the techniques of manipulating representations of material structures through digital tectonics has become a burgeoning part of the architectural knowledge base as well as one of its hottest research areas.

Fabricating Materiality: Design to Production and Back

The process of preparation for fabrication and construction depends upon a reinterpretation of the tectonics of the project. Frequently this is done by reuse of the digital core model of the project as Fabian Scheurer describes in his work on the digital production process for the formwork on the Mercedes-Benz Museum, Stuttgart by UNStudio and Werner Sobek (see Sobek's article on pp 24–33 of this issue).[16] Scheurer and designtoproduction have pioneered processes of digital tectonic description in support of both fabrication and conventional construction. The point here is that the tectonic data of the digital core model can function as information for the fabrication and construction processes. In a reversal of this process, it is possible that the tectonics of material systems can, in fact, drive the design process, a condition which is the epitome of architecture by performative design (see Neri Oxman's article on pp 78–85 of this issue).[17]

Design as Research

Among the motivating themes of design engineering is that design is a research-related and knowledge-producing process. The fields of structuring, digital tectonics, digital morphogenesis, materiality and performance-driven evolutionary generation are the research fields of the design engineer that are also common to the architect. This phenomenon is seen in the emergence in the last decade of interdisciplinary research groups such as the Arup Advanced Geometry Unit (AGU) which deal with the new range of geometric, computational and materialisation problems of contemporary design engineering practice.

Barkow Leibinger, 'Re-Sampling Ornament' exhibition, Swiss Architectural Museum, Basel, 2008
bottom: In these experiments in asymmetrical tube cutting by revolving 3-D cutting, new materialisation is achieved through fabrication potential. Tube arrays are studied as potential material technologies for architectural screen-walls.

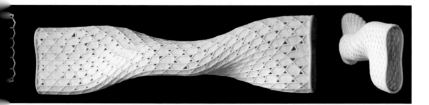

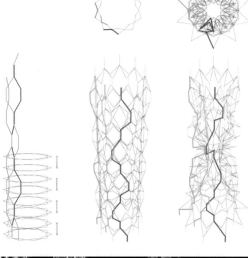

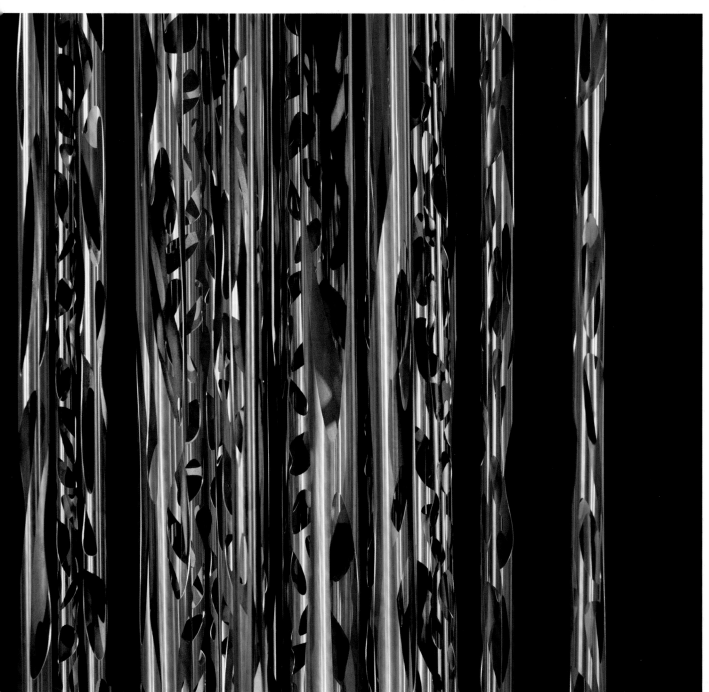

Neri Oxman, Beast: Prototype for a Chaise Longue,
Museum of Science, Boston, Massachusetts, 2009
opposite left: 'Form follows force', or the spontaneous generation of material
systems in response to environmental conditions, is a form of structuring without
formal preconceptions. This is the cutting edge of research-oriented practice in
what might become a technology of structuring in 'materialisation sciences' or
'material design sciences'. The drawings illustrate analytical procedures such as
pressure map registration eventually transformed into material form.

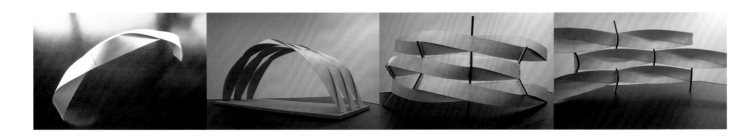

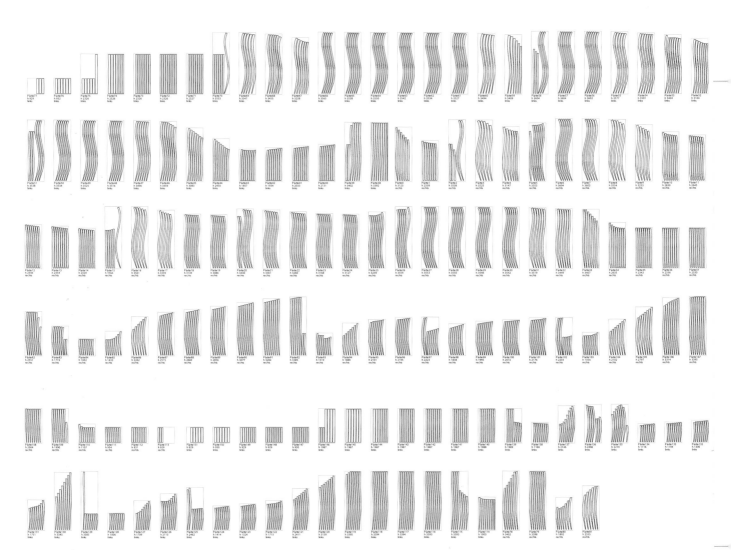

Fabian Scheurer, designtoproduction,
'Instant Architecture' travelling
exhibition, ETH Zurich, 2005
above: This project, and the
work of designtoproduction in
general, illustrates the manner in
which materiality is fabricated.
Materialisation and fabrication
become integrated as the idea of the
'component' is abandoned for the
concept of 'material system'.

Yves Weinand and Markus Hudert,
Timberfabric, IBOIS Laboratory,
EPFL, Switzerland, 2009–10
top: This group of works within the
Timberfabric research programme
explores experimental structural
morphologies of material in
processes uniquely integrating
material properties, engineering
and fabrication in the experimental
development of material systems.

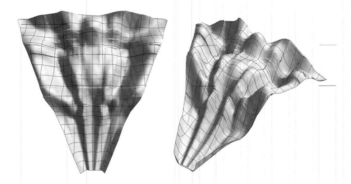

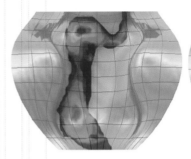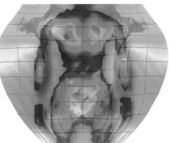

below: Point cloud density representation mapped from curvature.

From the Design of Engineering to the Re-Engineering of Design

We have proposed that design engineering is a new model of engineering methods and practice which also functions as a general model of design serving the architect as well as the structural engineer. It provides a head-clearing rationale to a profession beleaguered by the lightheadedness of form without matter.

How do we educate architects to function as material practitioners? What we have termed a 'cultural shift' obviously has a profound influence upon the definition of the requisite knowledge base of the architect as well as on what defines architectural research. Many of the research processes and subjects described above, including acquiring knowledge of architectural geometry and digital enabling skills, is already part of the agenda of the leading schools. Fabrication labs in education which were rare even just a few years ago are today commonplace.

Architecture's reconstitution as a material practice requires a theoretical foundation comprehensive enough to integrate emerging theories, methods and technologies in design, practice and education. The new structuralism is a first attempt to define this emerging paradigm viewed through the prism of engaging the structuring logic of design engineering and emerging technologies. The structuring, encoding and fabricating of material systems has become an area of design study and the expanded professional knowledge base common to both the architect and the structural engineer. The emergence of research practice is establishing the new design sciences of materialisation that are the threshold to the revolution of architectural technologies and material practice. The new structuralism focuses on the potential of these design processes to return architecture to its material sources. Architecture is, at last, back to the future. It may also be reformulating itself as a profession.

With the emerging technologies of fabrication, the current impact of material upon architectural form has become one of the prominent influences in architectural design. Fabrication is not a modelling technique, but a revolution in the making of architecture. The new structuralism designates the cultural turn away from formalism and towards a material practice open to ecological potential. This is an architectural design that is motivated by *a priori* structural and material concepts and in which structuring is the generative basis of design. This issue is devoted to the exegesis of this cultural turn in which the synthesis of architect, engineer and fabricator again controls the historical responsibility for the processes of design, making and building. ⚙

Notes

1. See Peter Rice, *An Engineer Imagines*, Artemis (London), 1998.
2. See Hanif Kara (ed), *Design Engineer-ing AKT*, Actar (Barcelona), 2008.
3. See Nina Rappaport, *Support and Resist: Structural Engineers and Design Innovation*, Monacelli Press (New York), 2007.
4. Among others, see: Cecil Balmond with Jannuzzi Smith, *Informal*, Prestel (Munich), 2002; Cecil Balmond, *Element*, Prestel (Munich), 2007; *a+u (architecture + urbanism)*, Special Issue: Cecil Balmond, November 2006; Michael Holm and Kjeld Kjeldsen (eds), *Cecil Balmond: Frontiers of Architecture* (exhibition catalogue), Louisiana Museum (Copenhagen), 2008.
5. Farshid Moussavi and Daniel Lopez-Perez, Seminar, 'The function of systems', *GSD Course Bulletin*, Harvard Graduate School of Design (Cambridge, MA), 2009; see www.gsd.harvard.edu/people/faculty/moussavi/seminars.html.
6. See 'Advanced Geometry Unit at Arup', in Tomoko Sakamoto and Albert Ferré et al, *From Control to Design: Parametric/Algorithmic Architecture*, Actar (Barcelona), 2008, pp 34–67.
7. See Mutsuro Sasaki, *Morphogenesis of Flux Structures*, AA Publications (London), 2007, pp 6, 81–99, 105.
8. See Martin Kemp, 'The natural philosopher as builder', in Michael Holm and Kjeld Kjeldsen, op cit, pp 90–9; and Irene Hwang, Tomoko Sakamoto, Albert Ferré, Michael Kubo, Noorie Sadarangi, Anna Tetas, Mario Ballesteros and Ramon Prat, *Verb Natures*, Actar (Barcelona), 2006.
9. See Julian Vincent, 2009, 'Biomimetic Patterns in Architectural Design', *AD Patterns of Architecture*, Nov/Dec 2009, pp 74–81.
10. See Lars Spuybroek (ed), *The Architecture of Variation: Research and Design*, Thames & Hudson (London), 2009.
11. Judith Reitz and Daniel Baerlecken, 'Interlacing systems', in Christoph Gengnagel (ed), *Proceedings of the Design Modeling Symposium Berlin*, University of Arts Berlin, 2009, pp 281–90.
12. See Rivka Oxman, 'Theory and Design in the First Digital Age', *Design Studies*, Vol 27, No 3, May 2006, pp 229–66; Rivka Oxman, 'Morphogenesis in the theory and methodology of digital tectonics', in René Motro (ed), *Special Issue of the IASS journal*, August 2010.
13. See Tomoko Sakamoto and Albert Ferré et al, op cit.
14. See Mutsuro Sasaki, op cit, especially pp 102–9.
15. Among others, see: Michael Hensel, Achim Menges and Michael Weinstock, *AD Emergence: Morphogenetic Design Strategies*, May/June 2004; and Michael Hensel, Achim Menges and Michael Weinstock, *AD Techniques and Technologies in Morphogenetic Design*, March/April 2006.
16. See also Fabian Scheurer, 'Fromdesigntoproduction', in Tomoko Sakamoto and Albert Ferré et al, op cit, pp 160–193.
17. See also Neri Oxman, 'Material computation', doctoral dissertation, MIT Department of Architecture, June 2010.

Text © 2010 John Wiley & Sons Ltd. Image: pp 14-15 © Bollinger + Grohmann, Matthias Michel; pp 16-17(t) © Arup; p 16(b) © Werner Sobek, Germany; p 18 © Barkow Leibinger Architects; p 19 © RWTH Aachen University, B Baerlecken and J Reitz; pp 20, 21(tr) © AKT; p 21(b) © Amy Barkow/Barkow Photo; p 22(t) © Markus Hudert/IBOIS EPFL; p 22(b) © Fabian Scheurer; p 23 © Neri Oxman

RADICAL SOURCES OF DESIGN ENGINEERING

Helmut Jahn and Werner Sobek, Post Tower, Bonn, 2003
The Post Tower has a height of 162 metres (531.4 feet) and is marked by its highly dematerialised building envelope.

The German architect and structural engineer, **Werner Sobek** is internationally renowned for his expertise in lightweight structures – an approach that is epitomised by the dramatic elegance of his glazed House R128. Here, Sobek explains how his practice has extended a highly specialised focus on ultra-lightweight facades to that of building structures, facade planning, and sustainable and low-energy solutions, interweaving research and innovation with design and consultancy work.

Werner Sobek, House R128,
Stuttgart, Germany, 2000
opposite: R128 is a fully glazed four-
storey building which is completely
recyclable. Moreover, it produces no
emissions and is self-sufficient in terms
of its energy requirements. It is thus
the first example of the Triple Zero
principle developed by Werner Sobek.

below: R128 is the first building
in which diametrical views and
outlooks through the building
are possible across four storeys.

The development that has taken place in the Werner Sobek
office over the last 17 years mirrors the changes that have taken
place in the practice's understanding of planning and design.
Where services were initially offered as highly specialised
designers and structural design engineers in the field of ultra-
lightweight facades, this soon extended to the '*in toto*' design
of building structures, and within just a few years to include
facade planning. It was vital to overcome the interface between
the load-bearing structure and the facade, which taken together
make up approximately 40 to 60 per cent of a building. The
next logical step was to extend the firm's expertise in the fields
of energy saving and recycling-friendly design, and to aim
to improve the emission characteristics of buildings with the
founding of subsidiary company WS Green Technologies.

Interwoven with this evolution of design engineering
praxis has been the related orientation to research and
experimentation carried out through the medium of an
academic chair and the leadership of the Institute for
Lightweight Structures and Conceptual Design (ILEK) at
the University of Stuttgart. It is this duality of involvement
that has enabled the firm to continuously refine and redefine
the radical principles of design engineering.

Transparency

The design of housing is continually used by the practice to
further develop its architectural concepts and underpin these
with engineering advances. House R128 in Stuttgart (2008) is
just such an experiment.[1] It is an attempt to comprehend the
archi-/structural nature of three-dimensional transparency.
The significance of R128 is to be found in the fact that
transparency has here for the first time been achieved and
experimented with in the third dimension, beyond the
prismatic precedents of Mies van der Rohe and Philip
Johnson. It is the first building in which interpenetrating
sight lines are possible across four storeys.

Christoph Ingenhoven and Werner
Sobek, European Investment Bank,
Luxembourg, 2007
below: The entire 11 storeys are covered
by a glass envelope so that large atriums
are created between the seven wings
making up the basic structure. Unlike
the large vertical cable-stayed front
facade, the completely glazed roof
structure is continuously curved at the
northwest side of the building.

Christoph Ingenhoven and Werner Sobek,
Lufthansa Aviation Center, Frankfurt, 2005
opposite top: The 10 fingers of the building
are roofed by double-curved reinforced
concrete shells. The atriums lying between
the fingers are roofed by double-curved
glazed steel-grid shells. The cable-stayed
facades of the atriums are up to 25 metres
(82 feet) high and can be deflected by
up to 400 millimetres (15.7 inches)
under wind load.

Helmut Jahn and Werner Sobek,
Post Tower, Bonn, 2003
opposite bottom: The tower is
enveloped by means of a second-skin
facade. This allows windows to be
opened even on the upper levels, and
forms an integral part of the energy
concept of the building, which is
based on minimal energy inputs.

In order to experiment with three-dimensional transparency and to experience its experiential and psychological attributes, the house was built as a personal lived-in experiment. Such a level of transparency can also be built on a large scale.[2] The architect Christoph Ingenhoven has proven this time and again with his work: particularly significant examples of this are the European Investment Bank in Luxembourg (2007) and the Lufthansa Aviation Center in Frankfurt (2005). The Lufthansa building is located in a very difficult urban environment between the airport, railway, dual carriageway and motorway. Despite this, all of the offices are open, flooded with daylight, naturally ventilated and offer wonderful views of the green inner courtyards. In this case the ideal of transparency is not restricted to the building envelope, but is continued throughout the inside of the building providing open, communicative structures that encourage interaction. These attributes also apply to the Post Tower in Bonn designed by Helmut Jahn (2003). The offices in this high-rise building are open to views of the surrounding area; it is possible to open windows on every level to allow fresh air into the rooms. These are examples of the experiential and environmental attributes of transparency.[3]

A fundamental research question is: How does transparency relate to other design engineering principles that ultimately contribute to ecological design? Werner Sobek seeks to build structures that do not consume fossil fuels, do not generate any emissions and are completely recyclable. All of these things should belong to the fundamentals of designing; a point that also applies in particular to higher education at our universities, just as much as questions of structural stability, facade technologies and so on.

Lightweight

Lightweight constructions are a precondition for transparency. Lightweight construction means the dematerialisation of objects, to optimise weight to the limit of the possible, reducing integrated grey energy.[4] The search for lightweight constructions is the search for boundaries. Designing the lightest possible constructions can be equated with feeling one's way towards the limits of what is physically and technically possible. It is about the aesthetics and physics of the minimal, and it is about stepping across the dividing lines between scientific disciplines. As far as constructions that bridge long span widths, reach great

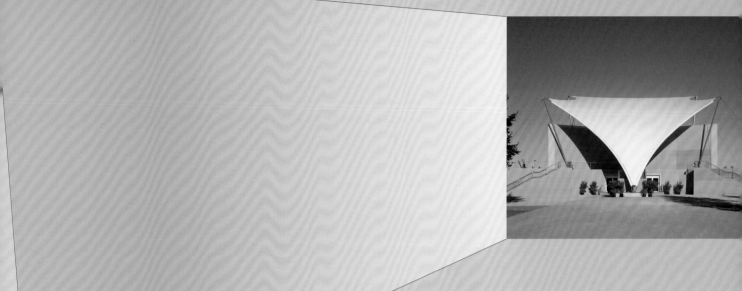

heights or move are concerned, reduction of self-weight load is an economic necessity and is also often the precondition for physical implementation. Irrespective of scale, lightweight design means savings on the mass of material deployed, and for the most part, also with regard to the amount of energy used. It is here that the ecological aspect begins: building light becomes a theoretical and ethical position.

A resolute approach to lightweight constructions requires modifications to the traditional structures of the design process. Establishing system geometries, forming and proportioning load-bearing structures as well as the selection of materials must primarily adhere to the requirement to save weight with other requirements taking on secondary importance; for example, those resulting from architectural considerations or from manufacturing techniques. Moreover, it is not possible to create a design of structural systems of minimal weight on the basis of a simple addition of the geometrically determined building components such as supports, balconies, arches, slabs, shear walls and so on. It is much more the case that the architect or engineer creating a lightweight construction designs spatial force paths, in other words, purely statically conditioned structures, for which he or she subsequently selects suitable materials.

Thus the logic of lightweight building is a radical, or fundamental, principle for ecological design.[5]

One example of researching the boundaries of extreme lightweight construction is the glass dome developed for the ILEK building (2005). The 8.5-metre (27.8-foot) diameter dome consists of glued panes of glass of just 10-millimetre (0.39-inch) thickness. In other words, the ratio of thickness to the span is 1:850. Other examples include the canopy developed for the pope's visit to Munich (2006) and the building envelope for Station Z in Sachsenhausen (2005), the latter having been created by the Stuttgart architect HG Merz. The membrane facade planned by Werner Sobek for Station Z is stabilised by a vacuum – an example of creative building with energy.

Geometry

In discussing new structures, the question posed is: What is 'new'? Developing force conditions has nothing to do with lining up basic, geometrically determined building blocks. The task is much more about developing structures that are nothing other than the materialisation of three-dimensional, perfectly designed systems of forces. This is the only possible way to obtain structures that have a high level of structural logic and make very

Werner Sobek, Papal Baldachin, Munich, 2006
opposite: On the occasion of his first official visit to Germany, in September 2006, Pope Benedict XVI celebrated a Mass in front of more than 250,000 pilgrims near the New Munich Trade Fair Center. The altar was roofed by a filigree membrane structure to protect him against possible rainfall.

Dr Lucio Blandini, Glass Cupola, Institute for Lightweight Structures and Conceptual Design (ILEK), Stuttgart, 2005
above: This prototype of a frameless structural glass shell was designed to demonstrate the structural efficiency as well as the aesthetic quality to be achieved by combining glass as the structural material with adhesives as the joining system. The shell spans 8.5 metres (27.8 feet) and is assembled by gluing only 10-millimetre (0.39-inch) thick spherical glass panes at the edges.

HG Merz and Werner Sobek, Station Z, Sachsenhausen, Germany, 2005
below: To protect the remains of the crematorium of the Sachsenhausen concentration camp, a protective shelter was erected in the form of a translucent envelope structure with a homogeneous surface. The roof was designed and built as a membrane structure stabilised by a partial vacuum.

Irrespective of scale, lightweight design means savings on the mass of material deployed, and for the most part, also with regard to the amount of energy used.

**Ben van Berkel (UNStudio) and
Werner Sobek, Mercedes-Benz
Museum, Stuttgart, 2006**
The Mercedes-Benz Museum
is not only a tribute to one of
the leading car manufacturers
in the world, but also a unique
demonstration of what structural
engineering may achieve today.
There are virtually no right angles
or plane surfaces in the whole
building, which was planned
completely in 3-D.

efficient use of materials. Consequently, they radiate a very special form of inherent beauty.[6]

Designing engineering is about the design of the three-dimensional flow of forces whose design space is dictated by architectural, climatic or other conditions. It is only after these force conditions have been optimised as much as possible that the designer turns to materialising the force fields with the material most suited to the task. For two-dimensional designs this is purely a finger exercise, but a huge amount of effort and creativity is required when such design is undertaken for three-dimensional structural integration.

New structures frequently involve innovative geometries. In this context, however, it is not simply a matter of optimising the building from an architectural point of view, but also from the standpoints of creating energetic structural planning and production techniques. If this is not accomplished, the resulting buildings tend rather to represent aesthetically motivated endeavours potentially limited in their habitability or usability.

Working with double-curved structures, or with biomorphic structures or bubble systems, requires a deep understanding of analytical geometry. This alone provides the basis from which it is possible to make assessments regarding the feasibility of producing the structures, as well as with regard to special issues of the building process. The Mercedes-Benz Museum in Stuttgart (2006) is an example of the structural and materialisation conditions of complex geometrical structures.[7] The double-curved, exposed concrete surfaces were created using a large number of formwork panels, each with a different border, produced utilising a water-jet cutting process to a tolerance of less than 1 millimetre (0.039 inches). The formwork panels were curved on site and provided a faceted surface.

Sustainability

If aspects of sustainability and recycling are integrated with complex geometries and dematerialised structures, the necessity for new tools and methods becomes imperative. Building must make huge changes in the face of rapidly accelerating urbanisation, the induced consumption of energy and the resulting emissions. We have simply neglected to develop the appropriate answers to these problems through research and to develop the tools and methods with which to create the solutions. Today, very few succeed in building structures that fulfil the simple demands required to achieve a Triple Zero rating (zero energy consumption, zero emissions (not just CO_2) and zero waste creation).

First examples such as R128, and House D10 which is currently being planned, are experimentally pushing the production of tools in the realisation of ecological values. It is now necessary to take a holistic view of building and design processes, considering the entire life cycle and beyond. If the components of a building are analysed, it can quickly be concluded that the load-bearing structure has a life cycle of 50

The imperatives of sustainability will lead to fundamental change in the traditional relationships between architects and structural design engineers, and other engineering and management consultants.

years and more; while in facade technology a generation cycle is significantly less than 30 years, and in technical building services the generation cycles are even shorter. Consequently, buildings should be designed in a manner that allows the individual components to be removed and replaced more easily as their various service life-cycles dictate.

The imperatives of sustainability will lead to fundamental change in the traditional relationships between architects and structural design engineers, and other engineering and management consultants. Putting sustainability into practice requires that each individual design engineer takes into consideration complex interrelating issues such as maintenance, repair and recycling. It requires the complete integration of aspects such as energy saving, emissions reduction and more. This cannot be achieved with the sequential planning processes as currently practised. We need to institutionalise new approaches to integral, cross-disciplinary design processes.[8]

This might enable those of us in new integrated teams of the design engineering professions to undertake a comprehensive examination of all relevant aspects of significance for a building and its users across its entire life cycle. It would then be possible to dedicate ourselves to the most important challenges for this century's architects and engineers: to make ecology breathtakingly attractive and exciting. ⌂

Notes
1. Werner Blaser and Frank Heinlein, *R128 by Werner Sobek*, Birkhäuser (Basel), 2001.
2. Frank Heinlein and Maren Sostmann, *Werner Sobek: Light Works*, AVEdition (Ludwisburg), 2008.
3. Werner Sobek, 'Engineered glass', in Michael Bell and Jeannie Kim (eds), *Engineered Transparency: The Technical, Visual, and Spatial Effects of Glass*, Princeton Architectural Press (New York), 2009, pp 169–82.
4. Werner Sobek and P Teuffel, 'Adaptive lightweight structures', in JB Obrebski (ed), *Proceedings of the International IASS Symposium* on *'Lightweight Structures in Civil Engineering'*, Warsaw, 24–28 June 2002, pp 203–10.
5. Werner Sobek, Klaus Sedlbauer and Heide Schuster, 'Sustainable building', in Hans-Jörg Bullinger (ed), *Technology Guide. Principles – Applications – Trends*, Springer (Heidelberg), 2009, pp 432–35.
6. Adolph Stiller (ed), *Skizzen für die Zukunft. Werner Sobek – Architektur und Konstruktion im Dialog.* Müry Salzmann (Vienna), 2009.
7. Susanne Anna, (ed), *Archi-Neering: Helmut Jahn and Werner Sobek*, Hatje Cantz (Ostfildern), 1999.
8. Conway Lloyd Morgan, *Show Me the Future: Engineering and Design by Werner Sobek*, AVEdition (Ludwigsburg), 2004.

Text © 2010 John Wiley & Sons Ltd. Images: pp 24, 29(t) © HG Esch; pp 26-7, 32 © Roland Halbe; pp 28, 29(b) © Andreas Keller; pp 30, 31(b) © Zooey Braun photography; p 31(t) © ILEK

Klaus Bollinger
Manfred Grohmann
Oliver Tessmann

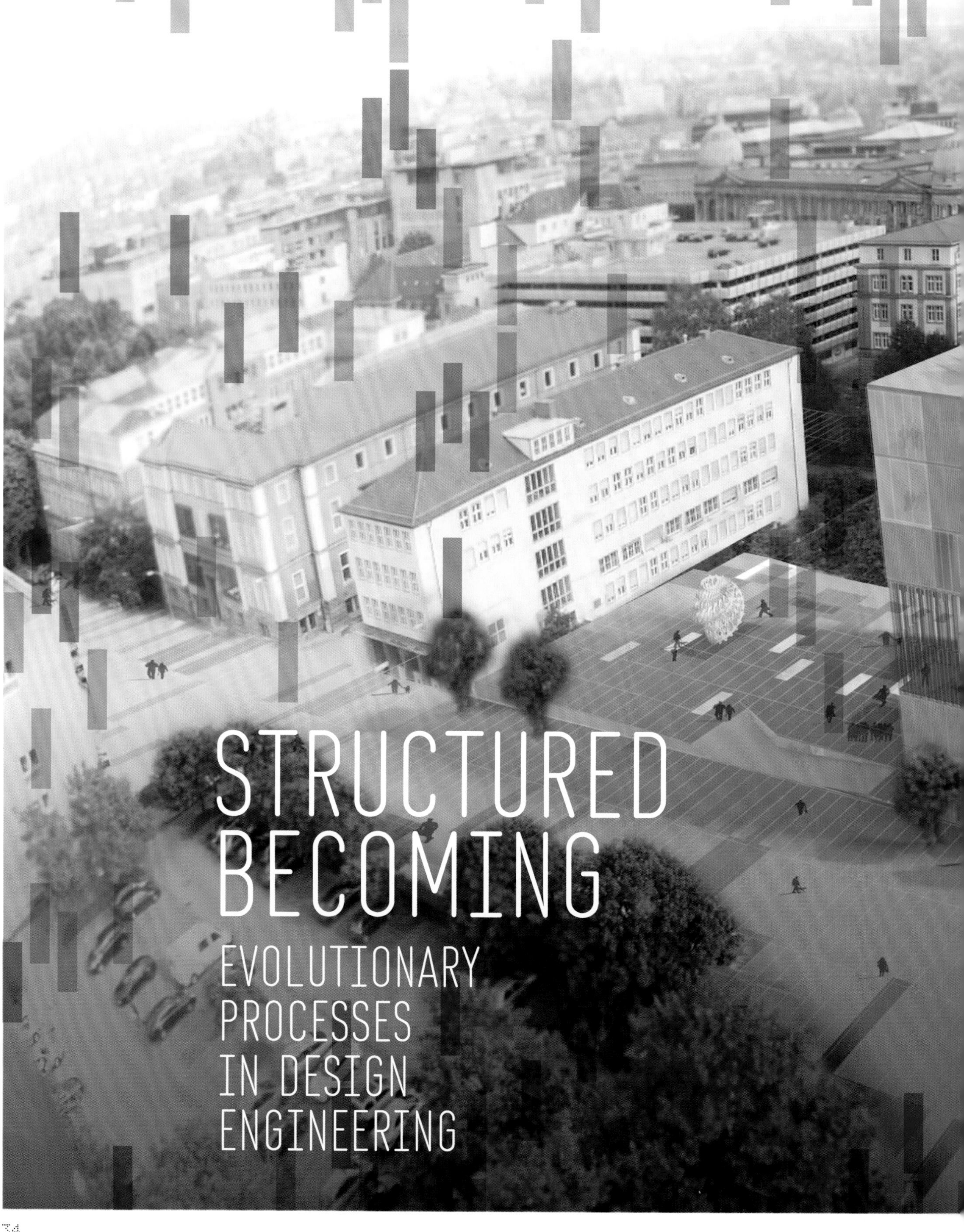

STRUCTURED BECOMING

EVOLUTIONARY PROCESSES IN DESIGN ENGINEERING

Computational design techniques are changing the role of analysis tools in collaborations between architects and engineers. Digital feedback loops of synthesis, analysis and evaluation establish a 'process of becoming' in which structural solutions evolve and adapt to specific requirements. Highly differentiated constructions are possible when digital techniques are fully integrated in design and production. **Klaus Bollinger, Manfred Grohmann and Oliver Tessmann** discuss these novel paradigms in relation to recent projects from engineering office Bollinger + Grohmann.

LAVA, VOxEL, Extension for the Hochschule für Technik, Stuttgart, 2009
Escape routes spiral along the facade and expand to balconies.

LAVA, VOxEL, Extension for
the Hochschule für Technik,
Stuttgart, 2009
Three diagrams describe the
major concept of the VOxEL
building: 1) A bitmap displays
areas of different densities; 2)
Stacked boxes define a void; 3)
Programme distribution within
a three-dimensional grid.

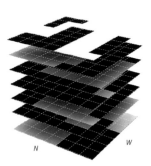

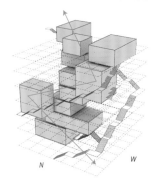

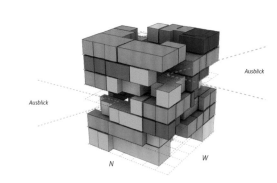

Complexity characterises systems – sets of elements and their relations – whose behaviour is hardly predictable. The system properties are not defined by individual elements, but rather emerge from intricate interaction without any top-down control. In structural design analysis, the prediction of structural behaviour is complemented by synthesis, which means that not only analytical but also generative strategies are required. Collaborative design of architects and engineers furthermore demands the embedding of structural design in a larger system with an increasing number of elements and relations. At Bollinger + Grohmann the resulting complexity is tackled by circular procedures regardless of whether they are digital or analogue. Instead of a linear cause–effect relationship, circularity creates feedback where effectors (output) are connected to sensors (input) that act with their signals upon the effectors. The computer becomes more than a mere calculating machine. Its formalised systems are not inscribed into mechanical cogwheels and step reckoners, but provided as a string of symbols based on a certain syntax. Scripting and programming help to access this layer of description where the algorithm (the machine) and the data are represented with similar symbols and syntax. These processes create the conditions for the digital mediation of design emergence through evolutionary structures, thus becoming characteristic of design engineering.

The Complexity of Evolving Structures

Evolutionary algorithms generate and manipulate character strings that serve as genotypes, or blueprints, of entire populations of structures. The genotype serves as input data for parametric structural models that become the phenotypes. Those structural individuals are successively analysed and evaluated. Evaluation criteria do not necessarily originate from structural requirements, but also cover architectural aspects. The goal is not an optimised structure but an equilibrium of multiple requirements. Successive generations are mainly based on the gene pool of the best solutions of the previous iteration. The individuals are reconfigured and mutated to generate a new set of various solutions. A cyclic process that takes the previous output as the new input is thus established.

LAVA, VOxEL, Stuttgart, 2009

An evolutionary algorithm was used in the competition for a new architecture faculty building in Stuttgart (2009) by the Laboratory for Visionary Architecture (LAVA) in collaboration with Bollinger + Grohmann. The proposal is based on a three-dimensional spatial continuum that provides a close interlocking of space, structure, voids and various functions. Beyond Le Corbusier's Maison Dom-Ino concept, the configuration offers flexibility across multiple levels.

The architectural and structural concept is based on a non-hierarchical organisation of floor slabs and shear walls proliferated into a three-dimensional matrix according to functional and structural requirements. The construction can be conceived as a square-edged sponge with continuously changing porosity. The shear walls resist lateral forces and replace a conventional structural core. Flexibility is thus gained in the third dimension.

The structural system developed in an evolutionary process. In a three-dimensional grid, every cell was mapped with one of two properties: cells free from any structure to provide voids for large spaces, or cells with a higher degree of subdivision and structural density.

Based on this preconceived setup, every grid cell was subsequently populated with a structural module consisting of two, one or no shear wall to create the square-edged sponge.

An initial generation of 50 random sponge versions was generated and analysed. Three evaluation criteria were used to rank the different solutions: vertical bending moments in the floor slabs under dead load; horizontal bending moments in the shear walls under lateral loads; and the placement of shear walls in relation to the cell property.

The configurations with the smallest bending moments and the best composition of shear walls according to the cell properties were used to generate offspring. Hence, the following generation was based on previously successful solutions. The recombination of the genotype (crossover) during reproduction and random mutation provided variation within the population.

After more than 200 generations, the process yielded a system that adapted to multiple architectural criteria while at the same time fulfilling the structural necessities.

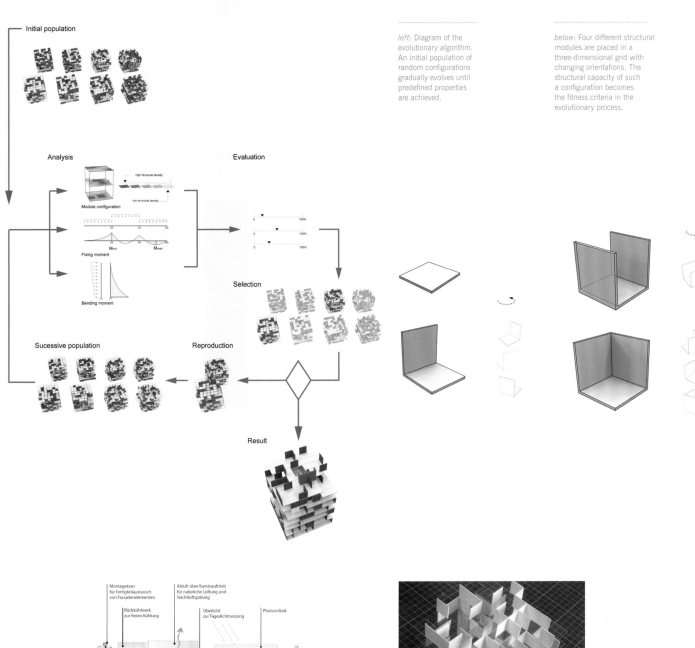

Initial population

Analysis

Module configuration

Fixing moment

Bending moment

Evaluation

Selection

Sucessive population

Reproduction

Result

left: Diagram of the evolutionary algorithm. An initial population of random configurations gradually evolves until predefined properties are achieved.

below: Four different structural modules are placed in a three-dimensional grid with changing orientations. The structural capacity of such a configuration becomes the fitness criteria in the evolutionary process.

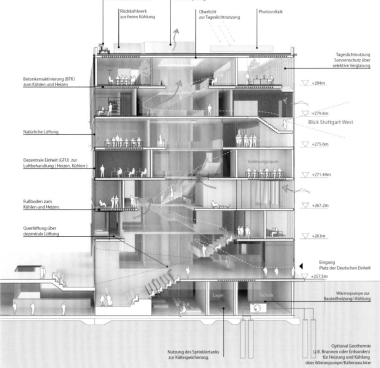

Montagekran
für Fertigteilaustausch
von Fassadenelementen

Abluft über Kaminauftrieb
für natürliche Lüftung und
Nachtluftspülung

Rückkühlwerk
zur freien Kühlung

Oberlicht
zur Tageslichtnutzung

Photovoltaik

Tageslichtnutzung
Sonnenschutz über
selektive Verglasung

Betonkernaktivierung (BTK)
zum Kühlen und Heizen

+284m

+279.8m
Blick Stuttgart West

Natürliche Lüftung

+275.6m

Dezentrale Einheit (GTU) zur
Luftbehandlung (Heizen, Kühlen)

Vorlesungsraum

+271.44m

+267.2m

Fußboden zum
Kühlen und Heizen.

Querlüftung über
dezentrale Lüftung

+263m

Eingang
Platz der Deutschen Einheit

+257.5m

Lager

Technik

Wärmepumpe zur
Bauteilheizung/-Kühlung

Nutzung des Sprinklertanks
zur Kältespeicherung.

Optional Geothermie
(z.B. Brunnen oder Erdsonden)
für Heizung und Kühlung
über Wärmepumpe/Kältemaschine

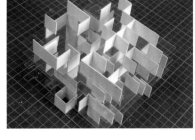

left: The programme revolves around a large void that serves as a communication space for all users.

above: Physical concept model of the square-edged sponge configuration.

Zaha Hadid Architects,
Hungerburgbahn,
Innsbruck, 2007
right: The structural system
is based on a series of ribs
that follow the curvature
of the skin. Asymmetric
support positions require a
central box-section profile
that resists torsion.

top: The
Hungerbahn
connects the
funicular with the
panorama cable-car
to the Nordkette
mountains.

middle: Curved steel
tubes served as the
mould for the glass
panels. A single layer
of glass was bent to
shape to provide a
continuous support
for the actual panel.

bottom: Every single
PE profile is labelled
to specify the position
in the structure.

The Complexity of Evolutionary Differentiation

The fact that computational design increases the complexity of geometry and CNC machines are able to fabricate such a non-standard architecture is well known. But it is now imperative in design engineering that the digital logic of evolutionary structuring must also be reflected in the material systems and the construction process.

In 1959 Konrad Wachsmann perceived the principles of industrialisation as similar to those of mass production. The benefit of automation is only attainable through quantity in production, a principle that distinguishes industrialisation from craftsmanship. To guarantee the sound assembly of mass-produced objects, Wachsmann introduced a system of modular coordination that defines the properties and quality of products. A superior universal module coordinates the different categories of modules such as geometry, tolerances, construction and so on. This industrial logic ensured constant and repeatable quality, but at the same time limited the range of what was buildable. Deviation from the idealised type is discarded and not seen as a possible solution.

The continuous digital workflow is comprised of similar elements of coordination but adapted to novel technological possibilities. The original within such a process is the generative algorithm. It produces data that is subsequently instantiated as G-code for milling or laser cutting, 3-D printing, rendering or drawing. Form is separated from the underlying principles that organise the relations of the different elements within the component. Every component can differ in geometry as long as the relations between its elements are correct. There is no ideal component and subsequent deviation.

The two different paradigms of industrial logic and digital fabrication became very obvious during the development of the glass fixings for the roof of Zaha Hadid's Hungerburgbahn cable-railway stations in Innsbruck, Austria (2007), where Bollinger + Grohmann was responsible for the structural design and the facade engineering. The connection of the steel structure and the double-curved glazed skin required a solution which embodies the logic of digital design and manufacturing.

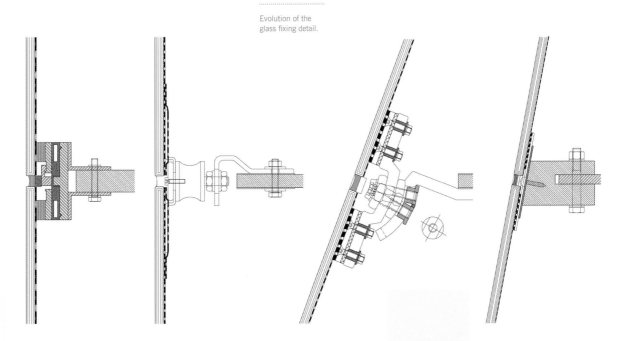

Evolution of the glass fixing detail.

Zaha Hadid Architects, Hungerburgbahn, Innsbruck, 2007
Four new stations of the cable railway connect Innsbruck city centre with the surrounding mountains. Every station has a free-formed glazed roof and solid concrete plinths. Although different in geometry, together they create a family with a highly recognisable formal language. The architectural goal was the creation of continuous, homogeneous surfaces without obtrusive joints and fixings. Only glass provided the desired surface qualities and thermal standards.

The double-curved float glass was coated from the inside with polyurethane resin, which accounts for the colour and also ensures a residual load-bearing strength in the event of breakage. The load-bearing structure consists of 8-millimetre (0.31-inch) and 12-millimetre (0.47-inch) vertical steel ribs with a depth of up to 3 metres (9.8 feet). The structure follows a series of cross sections of the skin with a spacing of 60 millimetres (2.36 inches) between the two.

A large effort was expended in the design of the glass–steel connection. The structural ribs were conceived as two-dimensional elements with a free-formed perimeter, but the glass fixings needed to follow the double curvature of the skin. The problem was at first approached with the logic of serial production. Brackets with flexible joints were proposed but the solution proved to be unfeasible. Such joints serve very well in absorbing tolerances, but here it would have been necessary to adjust every joint into a position that represented a three-dimensional coordinate and a tangential surface direction on the double-curved skin. The advantage of 18,000 similar brackets would have turned into a time-consuming disaster on site. Thus in the end the solution was provided by a simple continuous polyethylene profile which acts as a linear support for the glass panels. The profile is slotted and bolted to the steel ribs.

Since the upper face follows the double curvature of the glass skin, every single profile had to be milled individually. A continuous digital chain and a five-axis mill helped to cut the profile from sheet material and to minimise costs. The CNC data could be automatically derived from the 3-D model through specially developed software by designtoproduction

GmbH. The same custom application provided information for bolted connections, segmentation and nesting of profiles on the sheet material. Compact T-shaped sheet-metal elements were used for fixing the glass. Tight-fit screws could be placed anywhere on the polyethylene profiles which speeded up the assembly.

This combination of material polyethylene with digital design tools, specific software development and CNC fabrication proved to be most suitable to fulfil the demands of the project.

The Complexity Beyond Typology: Non-Linear Structures and Evolutionary Design

The glass fixing system of the Hungerburgbahn is an example of a typology that is derived from the entire population of elements rather than from a single condition. The aggregate-level concept of population thinking migrated into fabrication through the use of digital technologies. The VOxEL project refers to a paradigm shift in structural design driven by a conceptual use of digital techniques in every phase of design and construction. The finite element method (FEM) allows the examination of structures beneath the scale of parts that dissolves traditional structural engineering typological building blocks. Structural behaviour relies more on a network of interconnected elements than on simple structural typologies. Such an engineering approach improves the collaboration with architects and their surface models. Analysis data is fed back into the generative model and serves as a design driver rather than the basis for mere post-rationalisation. Thus the application of the phrase 'design engineering' to designate a highly interactive process of form generation and refinement between architects and engineers as diverse requirements are mediated between them is, in fact, a new and unique emerging paradigm of engineering design. ◮

Text © 2010 John Wiley & Sons Ltd. Images: pp 34-6, 36(b) © LAVA Stuttgart; pp 37(t), 38-9 © Bollinger + Grohmann Ingenieure

Wolf Mangelsdorf

STRUCTURING STRATEGIES FOR COMPLEX GEOMETRIES

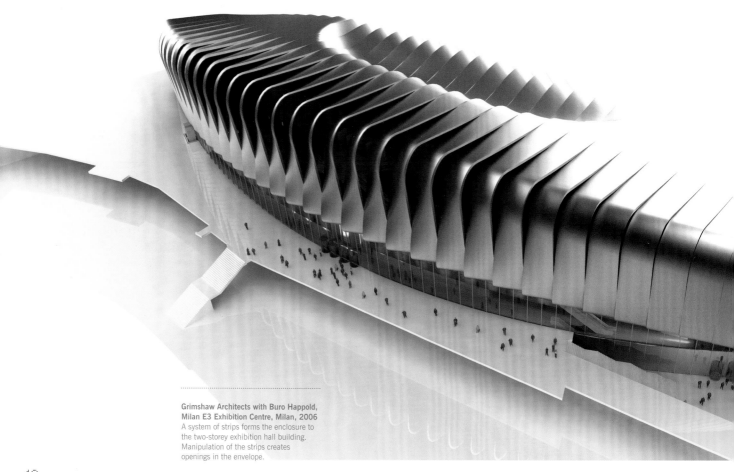

**Grimshaw Architects with Buro Happold,
Milan E3 Exhibition Centre, Milan, 2006**
A system of strips forms the enclosure to
the two-storey exhibition hall building.
Manipulation of the strips creates
openings in the envelope.

Over the last couple of decades, computation has proved a great facilitator for design, allowing far greater scope for analysis and generative design. Intelligent engineering, though, can only be truly set apart by the pursuit of the right design strategy, as outlined here by **Wolf Mangelsdorf** of Buro Happold. Mangelsdorf highlights four different models that enable the generation and engineering of geometrically complex forms and describes how they have been applied by Buro Happold in four very diverse projects with different architect collaborators.

The design of complex three-dimensional shapes is among the most interesting challenges for structural engineers. Irrespective of whether a structure is visible, it forms the skeleton for the architecture and the basis for geometric coordination. Design strategies are required for this intelligent engineering that embrace the inherent structural behaviours of such complex geometries from the start and allow the coordination of structure, architecture and fabrication. Studying their basic principles, communalities and differences, one can develop a classification of the different types of surfaces and geometries and derive from them the right modelling approaches.

While the computer has facilitated advances in the design and analysis of these types of structures, we are still using models that reflect more or less well the reality. Reduction and abstraction in these models are necessary, not least to limit the amount of data produced and to keep control of outputs. Choosing the right model approach is therefore of great importance and, with some simplification, we can derive four different categories for the generation and engineering of geometrically complex forms:

Form-Finding

Form-finding refers to the design of engineered minimal surfaces – doubly curved tension or compression structures – based on physical constraints. It is prominent in many of the projects that Buro Happold has completed with Frei Otto, and produces very distinctive and highly efficient structures for large-scale lightweight enclosures. Defined by internal and external forces, these kinds of surfaces are shaped through a manipulation of the boundary conditions. The aesthetics of such force-defined geometries are therefore directly related to physics – placing great demands on the collaboration between the engineer and architect.

Simple Mathematical Geometry

This category refers to complex geometries that are based on basic mathematical geometries: sphere, cylinder, torus, line, circle, ellipse. These are comparatively simple to handle in a computer model, which is why this design approach is found in many examples of doubly curved surface structures designed with the 3-D CAD software tools that emerged in the mid-

and late 1990s. Being ideal for a parametric description of the geometry, their other big advantage is the straightforward translation of the design into built form, allowing complex shapes to be constructed with basic straight or bent elements. The engineering itself is dependent on the shape and often related to systems of doubly curved lattice surfaces with predominantly planar forces and a minor element of bending.

Free Form

Free form as a concept describes development of the form independent or either physical constraints or the limitations of the simple mathematical geometries. Subsequently, there is nothing that can initially guide the structural engineering design. Its coordination with the geometry requires an intelligent concept that can vary in every instance. The engineering designer must interpret the form and apply or invent and develop a structural logic. Developing the right concepts with the architect so that a solution is found where form and structure meet without the loss of the basic underlying idea is crucial. However, where a consistent engineering logic cannot be developed out of the given form, the resulting compromises have a serious negative impact on the architecture.

Hybrid Approaches

One way around the inherent limitations to the engineering of total free form is a solution which brings together aspects of all three of the above-mentioned methods. It allows a high degree of freedom in the development of the form, but integrates concepts based on physics, form description and fabrication. The compromises of this approach need to be tested against the initial concepts, requiring a high degree of coordination and trust between architect and engineer. However, the great advantage is that any solution based on this approach will have a conceptual integrity that unifies architectural form and engineering solution.

Recent examples, explored in the following in some more detail, help illustrate these four different approaches, demonstrating how the characteristics of each project influences the choice of design route, and how the design philosophy is giving the projects strong and recognisable identities.

Frei Otto with Ted Happold
(Ove Arup & Partners),
Multihalle Mannheim
Hanging Chain Model, 1975
below left: Hanging
chain model used for the
development of the geometry
for the timber grid-shell.

Foster + Partners with Buro
Happold, Sage Music Centre,
Gateshead, 2004
bottom left: Build-up of the
geometry based on a series of
interconnected torus surfaces.

Ushida Findlay with
Buro Happold, Doha
Villa, Doha, Qatar, 2002
below right: Overlay of
the different layers of
the free-form geometry
developed for the villa.

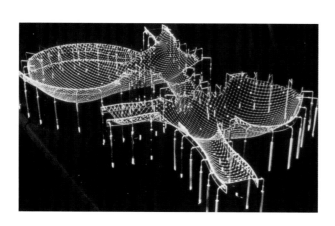

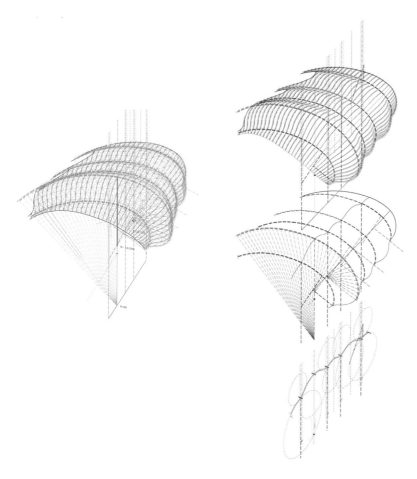

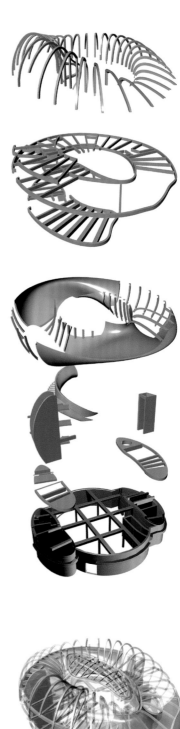

Foster + Partners with Buro
Happold, Smithsonian Institution,
Washington DC, 2007
The grid shell for the Smithsonian,
based on a system of quadrangles,
uses characteristics of form-found
geometry together with quite
unique boundary conditions –
single points of support and no
lateral restraints at its edges.

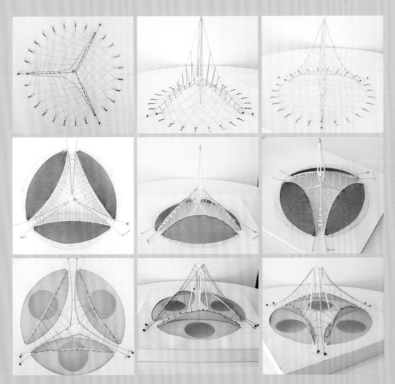

Form-Finding: Khan Shatyr
Entertainment Centre, Kazakhstan

For this large-scale entertainment centre, Foster + Partners and Buro Happold designed a transparent cone-shaped cable-net structure that rises over a reinforced buried concrete base that in turn forms the 200-metre (656-foot) diameter support ring to the main cables. Initial form-finding studies were based on the traditional approach using a series of hanging models to investigate the overall behaviour and to determine the final shape of the cable net. The chosen inclined cone shape was developed further using computer models that allowed the refinement of both the overall form and the layout of the cables themselves. The single central support mast is designed as a stable tripod that accommodates the movement of the cable net under different force conditions by means of a pivoting head. The ethylene tetrafluoroethylene (ETFE) cladding to the cable net makes maximum use of the transparency that this kind of structure allows, having no requirement for a smaller glazing grid and being flexible enough to be compatible with the comparably large expected movement of this tensile structure. Self-supporting foil cushions with spans of approximately 4 metres (13 feet) are mounted directly onto the main cables. The project is due for completion at the end of 2010.

Foster + Partners with Buro
Happold, Khan Shatyr Entertainment
Centre, Kazakhstan, 2010
A series of physical models was
used to develop the structure for the
cable net, exploring various cable
arrangements. The chosen scheme
was then taken forward and analysed
in specialist computer software.

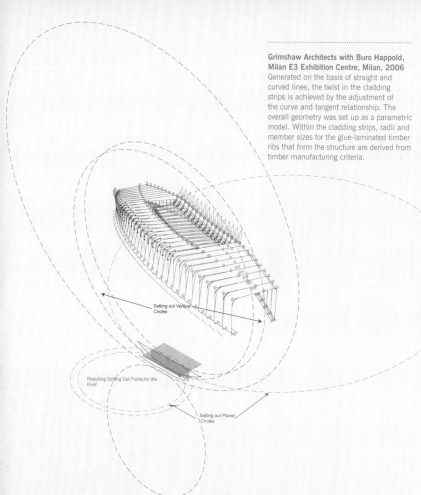

Grimshaw Architects with Buro Happold,
Milan E3 Exhibition Centre, Milan, 2006
Generated on the basis of straight and
curved lines, the twist in the cladding
strips is achieved by the adjustment of
the curve and tangent relationship. The
overall geometry was set up as a parametric
model. Within the cladding strips, radii and
member sizes for the glue-laminated timber
ribs that form the structure are derived from
timber manufacturing criteria.

Simple Mathematical Geometry:
Milan E3 Exhibition Centre

For a new exhibition centre in Milan, Grimshaw Architects
and Buro Happold developed the envelope using parallel
zinc-clad strips based on a simple structural and geometrical
concept. With just straight and curved lines and using only
a minimum number of different radii, each of the strips
was manipulated to form openings and twists. The team
used a parametric modelling approach integrated with the
structural analysis of the strips, allowing the aesthetics
and the engineering of the surface to be investigated in
an iterative development. The structural material, glue-
laminated timber ribs acting as a series of beams supported
off the exhibition halls, proved cost effective and produced
the desired internal finishes. In discussions with timber
manufacturers, key material constraints (length, radii,
connections) were determined early on and integrated
within the design. The project, which to date has not
been realised, demonstrates how the integration of simple
geometrical rules derived from cost and material constraints
can lead to the most creative manipulation of geometry.

Zaha Hadid Architects with Buro
Happold, Glasgow Museum of Transport,
Glasgow, due for completion 2011
above: Complex nodes were
manufactured off site allowing the
connections between individual structural
elements to be simple. The roof was
assembled as a kit of prefabricated parts.

Free Form: Glasgow Museum of Transport

The Glasgow Museum of Transport project started as a design
competition for a new building to replace an existing museum.
For its location, a former industrial river-front site, Zaha Hadid
Architects in collaboration with Buro Happold developed a
concept of a large multiridge roof with column-free spaces,
S-shaped on plan. Flanked by accommodation, the roof encloses
the main exhibition hall with two large glazed facades at the
city and river ends. Directly spanning across the 30-metre (98-
foot) wide space was not compatible with the geometry. The
building form provided the alternative: to span the long way
and to use the inclined planes of the roof as folded plates. This
concept, developed during the competition stage, and realised
as a series of inclined trusses rigidly connected to each other
at ridge and valley lines, has been the basis for the structural
design throughout the project. Facade mullions provide vertical
support at either end of the building. At the transition between
straight parts of the folded plate structure the engineering again
intelligently uses the geometry: the roof planes are a series
of convex and concave shells that are interlocked and create
a stiff strip spanning across the roof. The Glasgow Museum
of Transport is a clear example where a free from could be
elegantly used as a structure, by seeing and understanding the
opportunities the architectural shape offered. The early concepts
have been developed to construction level, and the building is
currently on site with the structure completed and fully clad,
and due to open to the public in 2011.

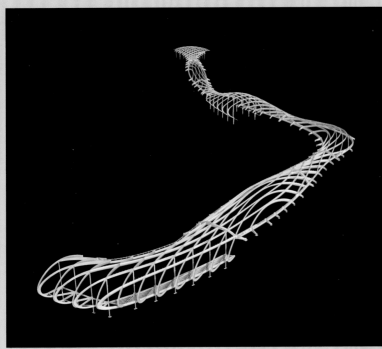

Ron Arad Associates with Buro
Happold, Médiacité Liège, Liège, 2009
left top: The parametric model, which
was later refined and fully coordinated
with the engineer's and the contractor's
3-D models, took the initial design
ideas and developed them into a
scheme that could be manipulated
according to architectural design
development, boundary conditions and
engineering criteria.

left bottom: The realised
structure had undergone a series
of engineering optimisations,
including from the construction
criteria developed with the
manufacturer. The end result
still reflects exactly the
architect's design intent.

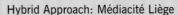

Hybrid Approach: Médiacité Liège

The roof structure for Médiacité in Liège (Ron Arad
Associates with Buro Happold) was developed with a
clear architectural and engineering idea using physical
form-finding and a mathematical description of the
structural elements for the optimisation of the geometry.
The design is based on a series of intersecting ribs that
form one consistent concept for the entire 400-metre
(1,312-foot) length of the roof and are used as the
structure. The roof is clad in ETFE, underlining the
ribs as the main solid elements and secondary structure.
In a form-finding exercise, the shell action of the roof
was increased where possible. Reducing the number of
ribs, as well as their depth and size, and also integrating
the requirements and suggestions of the manufacturer,
significantly reduced the weight and therefore the cost of
the steelwork without any detriment to the architecture.
The project opened to the public in October 2009.

To summarise: when designing complex three-
dimensional shapes and geometries, structural
engineering has to be a creative contribution to
the design process, so that a full integration and
coordination of aesthetical and physical aspects
can be achieved. This relies completely on the
development of engineering concepts that understand
and facilitate the design, and at the same time close
collaboration with the architect, manufacturer and
other design disciplines. The engineering modelling
and realisation strategies outlined here help to
create that important conceptual clarity behind
the development of the design – the basis of a
constructive dialogue between the design partners
and a trusting relationship between architect and
structural engineer. ◬

Text © 2010 John Wiley & Sons Ltd. Images: pp 40-1 © Grimshaw; p
42(tl) © Frei Otto; pp 42(bl&r), 44(t) © Buro Happold; p 43(t) © Buro
Happold, photo Timothy Hursley; p 43(b) © Buro Happold, photo Foster
+ Partners; p 44(b) © Zaha Hadid Architects; p 45(t) © Ron Arad
Associates; p 45(b) © Buro Happold

ON DESIGN ENGINEERING

London-based Adams Kara Taylor (AKT) is one of the most innovative design-led structural and civil engineering practices in the UK. Seeking out creative collaborations with leading architectural firms and schools of architecture and design internationally, it has, as **Hanif Kara**, Co-Founder and Director at AKT, explains, developed a holistic approach in which architecture and engineering converge. Here Kara defines the emerging methods of 'design engineering', emphasising the importance of early input at the conceptualisation stage and research over even the contribution of digital technologies.

Hanif Kara

The pioneering collaborations that the structural engineers Adams Kara Taylor (AKT) have sought out with cutting-edge architectural practices have given them a leading role in the formation of an interactive design approach. (Recent collaborators include Foreign Office Architects, Zaha Hadid Architects, Heatherwick Studio, Fielden Clegg Bradley, Foster + Partners, Will Alsop, Amanda Levete, BIG, AHMM and David Chipperfield.) With the firm's work being the subject of two recent monographs, *Design Engineering*[1] and *From Control to Design: Parametric/Algorithmic Architecture*,[2] and an exhibition, 'Adams Kara Taylor: AKT at Work' at the Architectural Association (AA) in London in 2009, AKT has begun to articulate a theoretical framework for the practice of architectural structural engineering.

The very use of the term 'design engineering' in the title of AKT's monograph suggests a consciously different approach to design collaboration between the architect and engineers. Design engineer is actually a common title in engineering offices, but its use as a verb here allows for multiple readings. It represents the expert discipline of engineering, but also a culture, an attitude and a practice that accommodates a joint discourse with other designers. This attitude emerges out of AKT's restlessness to contribute to design, as well as a curiosity to find new ways to relate engineering with other design practices. As architectural author and editor Michael Kubo writes in an introductory essay to the exhibition of AKT's work at the AA, the term 'conveys a double intent both to design new models of engineering and to engineer the practice of design itself'.[3] Rather than a service model in which the engineer simply rationalises the architect's forms, it is a strategic or empathetic model 'that requires inhabiting the mind of the architect … while thinking with the knowledge of the engineer'. This approach is a 'contrast to other contemporary models that seek to equate the engineer to the role of the architect, ignoring the real differences between them'.

While these ideas are influenced by past examples of collaboration between engineers and architects, the concept of design engineering has been structured to capture the last 10 years of AKT's practice, and in that sense there is little precedence. Engineering precedents can rely heavily upon a singular individuality, which is difficult to relate to this collaborative interpretation of engineering. Among current offices in the UK, the work of certain teams at Arup and Buro Happold may share the closest resemblance. This does not mean that contemporary engineers who specialise in a particular

Foreign Office Architects (FOA), Ravensbourne College, London, 2010
The facade of the college building creates an abstract pattern from floral shapes that introduces a geometrical order based on a tile unit. This affects not just the facade, but also determines the internal organisation, such as floor-to-ceiling heights and structural grids.

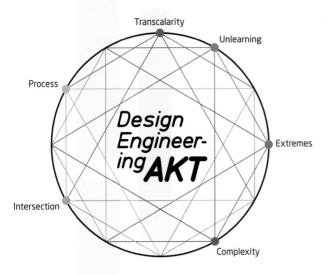

AKT instruments of Design Engineering

'Adams Kara Taylor: AKT at Work', Architectural Association (AA), London, 2009
left: AKT instruments of design engineering: recent themes in architecture that have gone through the office in the last decade.

opposite: The first-ever solo exhibition of projects by AKT as well as a commissioned installation built in the AA Gallery.

system, technical process or material (for example, Frei Otto in fabrics or Santiago Calatrava in concrete) are subordinate, but that the model of individuality is becoming less significant in the world of AKT's practice. As Kubo writes, the collaborative model suggests an approach that 'ideally has no fixed signature or style, but consists instead in the expertise it brings to bear on the diverse problems and formal languages of the architectures it makes possible. In this pluralistic model the engineer is neither wholly creator nor solely problem-solver but instead operates at their intersection, adopting different roles depending on the needs and working methods of each project.'

Design engineering practice is about developing a 'tool box' of procedural and methodological instruments. In AKT's first decade of work, process, complexity, trans-scalarity, extremes, unlearning and intersection were identified as instruments to avoid the traditional homogenising role of structural engineering in projects, and offer a legitimate adaptability to different starting points without devaluing technical expertise. This tool box is not developed in a void, but has grown from exposure to the projects, architects, clients, constructors and institutions with whom AKT has been fortunate enough to work. These instruments can only be labelled in retrospect, once projects have been constructed. The methods that emerge from this process are non-linear compared to institutional research models, since they stem simultaneously from technical know-how and a studio environment that seeks to innovate by responding to other designers' intentions, not just to a superficial understanding of new architectural forms.

There is no question that digital media have played a role in supporting and unifying such interactions as 'enabling technologies' that enhance the potential for communication and collaboration between architects and structural engineers. New tools of analysis and simulation that have been developed or adapted from other disciplines provide an ability to sharpen the iterative, collaborative nature of what the design engineer does, and so the evolution of digital design media has improved the engineering discipline significantly. But these new media should also be approached cautiously since the ubiquity of digital media cannot replace human interaction that frames new questions and permits interdisciplinary creativity.

Just as digital design tools must be approached with caution, it should also be noted that geometry and mathematics, while important, do not constitute a new lingua franca for this relation between architecture and engineering. While words, gestures and desires derived solely from geometry or mathematics may appear to produce coherent design and clearly articulated forms, realistically these may be anything but coherent, and can often be meaningless to those who use buildings and consume the work of architects and engineers. The gap in how to use and share knowledge is also still hazardous because of the segregation of disciplines into 'silos' and a lack of expertise. It is preferable to think of a passion for design that demonstrates value as a truer lingua franca, one that stimulates the engineer to find areas of compromise and operate within those zones.

Just as good architecture relies on good clients, good architects make for good engineering. They understand the basic technical role played by engineers, but can also push engineers to think of questions they have not thought of themselves. In this way, good architects know how to get the best out of engineers. For example, the design for Foreign Office Architects' Ravensbourne College in London (2010) is grounded as an extension of their research on facade patterns and ornament, but still required an unspoken empathy in order to subvert, yet still control, the structural and constructional aspects. Their latent control ensures that FOA's goals are kept in the foreground. Collaboration needs to be encouraged during the conceptualisation stage, rather than relying on structural gymnastics to 'hang' architecture on to, or on bringing in engineers later to make an architect's concept 'work'. Kubo writes that architects have often seen engineers as 'inspiration or competition, parallel practitioners with the means to formal innovation through structural and fabrication techniques that have often been beyond the capacities of architects themselves'. This attitude 'has enforced an artificial boundary that has been more concerned with deciding which concepts "belong" to one or the other, rather than exploring the territory between them'. For this reason, design engineering avoids the idea of innovation in engineering and stresses the broader idea of innovation in design, involving the expertise of the engineer. This subtle but important difference is perhaps the distinguishing characteristic

Structuring knowledge, such as
the use of geometry in developing
patterning and three-dimensional
structural morphologies, has
become an important part of
design engineering practice.

below: AKT
implemented a
glass-clad pavilion
with all-round
views for Overland's
London offices.

opposite: Value
zone diagram
describing the
zone that AKT
operates within to
search for design
opportunities.

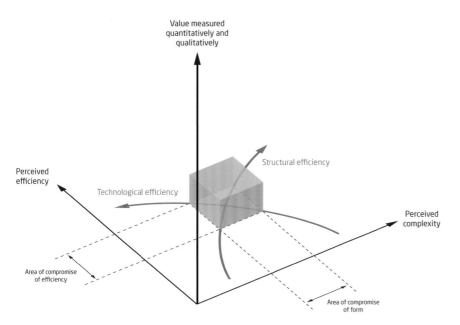

of collaborative design: the disciplinary contribution is integrated throughout the design, rather than residing in a particular system or element.

Personal interaction is also a factor in collaborating across design practices. Interacting with strong personalities requires the design engineer to be clear about intent, as authorship is a key issue. AKT is explicit that this always remains with the architect, and avoids taking any claim of joint authorship; its engineers prefer to act and be seen as 'disciplinary agents'. From this position the office is able to give back its best engineering, not bad architecture. This has enabled relationships that have been creative for everyone involved and which let the engineers be judged only for what they do best.

Structuring knowledge, such as the use of geometry in developing patterning and three-dimensional structural morphologies, has become an important part of design engineering practice. The building industry is often too quick to knock things down without any calibration on the basis of affordability or lack of precedent, so it is important to develop information through building as a benchmark for real knowledge. This is true, for example, of three-dimensional structural morphologies, which have a close relationship to natural systems, providing one is careful about scaling them. The successes and failures of the recent C Space Pavilion constructed at the AA in March 2008, on which AKT collaborated, provided a vast amount of knowledge in terms of collaboration, education, processes, material and costs.

Research is increasingly important as a mode of design engineering. To this end, AKT maintains a loose formation of interdisciplinary participants, called P.ART (Parametric Applied Research Team), that comes together on an ad hoc basis to conduct research in relation to projects. However, to claim P.ART as a research group is somewhat disingenuous. Scientific research is very different from architectural (re)search. When dealing with a 'hard core' problem like the reuse of an existing pile foundation or joint testing on long-span glass beams, tested with universities to reach a definitive answer, the evaluation criteria are clear. Design (re)search on the other hand is often difficult to measure; it can aim for completeness only in stages, not at the end. P.ART is therefore not a research

group per se, but comes from the need for a 'polydiscipline' that crosses interdisciplinary boundaries to improve the engineer's contribution, since each project has a different centre of focus. As Kubo notes, 'while this emphasis … is perhaps less visible in the results it makes possible, it is far more extensive in its impacts, since it is not limited to the production of one-off examples or signature forms'. The group is an 'idea' that affects all of AKT's work and focuses on pioneering ways of enabling and communicating both internally and externally.

The importance of research and the acquisition of new knowledge in design engineering interfaces naturally with an involvement in education. For example, the concept of design engineering relied in part on involvement in teaching a Diploma Unit with Ciro Najle at the AA, and on a supporting role with the Design Research Lab there. These formative years in education coincided with the formative years of AKT's work, and one has inevitably influenced the other. While there is a school of thought that educating from practice can blunt creativity, the involvement of AKT's practice with education comes from the opposite belief that the experience of the practitioner, combined with the inexperience of students, provides exactly the right extreme for the survival of design education as a form of knowledge. Architectural education has adapted to this mix between speculation and practice much better than engineering education, which in some ways is still in the dark ages – not in terms of what it teaches, but in the environment it provides for learning. Traditional roles are already changing and disciplinary labels will need to reflect this in the future. This can only happen through a change in education and a revolution in the institutions that dictate the current rules of engagement. ∆

Notes
1. Hanif Kara (ed), *Design Engineering: Adams Kara Taylor*, Actar (Barcelona), 2008.
2. 'P.ART at Adams Kara Taylor', in Albert Ferré and Tomoko Sakamoto (eds), *From Control To Design: Parametric/Algorithmic Architecture*, Actar (Barcelona), 2008, pp 116–59.
3. Michael Kubo, 'Engineering Models', in the pamphlet for the exhibition 'Adams Kara Taylor: AKT at Work', held at the AA School of Architecture in London from 19 January to 14 February 2009. All subsequent quotes are from this essay (no page numbers).

Text © 2010 John Wiley & Sons Ltd. Images: pp 46-7, 49, 51 © AKT; p 48 © Valerie Bennett; p 50 © Jan-Uwe Friedlein (AKT)

Julio Martínez Calzón
Carlos Castañón Jiménez

WEAVING ARCHITECTURE STRUCTURING THE SPANISH PAVILION, EXPO 2010, SHANGHAI

A complex basket-like structure woven from lightweight steel and wicker, the Spanish Pavilion for the Expo 2010, in Shanghai, is the site of a unique collaboration between architects EMBT (Enric Miralles and Benedetta Tagliabue) and MC2 Structural Engineers. Here **Julio Martínez Calzón and Carlos Castañón Jiménez** of MC2 describe how intense dialogue became key to the realisation of the pavilion, as form-finding and the development of the underlying structural system were equally integral to the design process.

EMBT (Enric Miralles/
Benedetta Tagliabue),
Spanish Pavilion, Expo
2010, Shanghai
Interior perspective:
woven space.

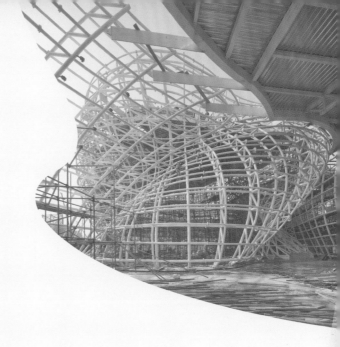

EMBT (Enric Miralles/
Benedetta Tagliabue),
Spanish Pavilion, Expo
2010, Shanghai
The pavilion under
construction.

The Spanish Pavilion for the Expo 2010 in Shanghai, China, was designed by the architectural firm EMBT (Enric Miralles/ Benedetta Tagliabue) in collaboration with MC2 Structural Engineers. Its complex geometry and lightweight 'virtual volume' generated by a steel framework and a wicker covering creates a fresh interpretation of the concept of the pavilion. Its objectives were to blend the primordial craft quality of weaving with the network structure, non-linearity and complex spatial vision of the future. Thus 'on weaving architecture' became a motif of this project that also seeks to weave the past into an architectural vision of the future.

This complex interpretation demanded a unique level of collaborative work on the part of the architects and engineers to optimise the idea within the framework of an integration of architectural and structural means. Current interest in the structural properties of complex meshes led to the search for means to accommodate new techniques in a mesh structure of such a high level of formal complexity. Woven architecture became a prerogative for weaving structure.

The highly irregular, strongly curved free form of EMBT's building is characterised by multiple complex curvatures that problematise design as a traditional structural form. The need to develop an adequate structural system that gave support to the free form of the building required an intense dialogue between architecture and engineering at the beginning and throughout the whole of the design and production cycles. Such a form of design engineering is itself an intensely interwoven fabric.

During the dialogue, the main variables which configure the building were considered in an attempt to find the structural system which best merged into the form to create a coherent structure. In this investigation of the 'tensibility' of the form, the double curvature of the enveloping facade was both a challenge and the solution to the structural system, as these shapes, when adequately configured, behave in an optimal structural way.

The structure was therefore created by means of a spatial double orthogonal layer of tubular grids which form the facades, taking advantage of the double curvature shape and enabling the building to respond to the required loadings – self-weight, live loads, wind, seismic forces – in an active structural way. The facades, inner columns, floors, roofs and bracing cores combine to form the overall structural system, which relies on the global collaboration and interaction of all of its parts to give

The highly irregular, strongly curved free form of EMBT's building is characterised by multiple complex curvatures that problematise design as a traditional structural form.

EMBT (Enric Miralles/
Benedetta Tagliabue),
Spanish Pavilion, Expo
2010, Shanghai
Interior perspective:
materialisation of
the concept.

EMBT (Enric Miralles/
Benedetta Tagliabue),
Spanish Pavilion, Expo
2010, Shanghai
below: Conceptual model.

bottom: Conceptual
model: spatial and
structural components.

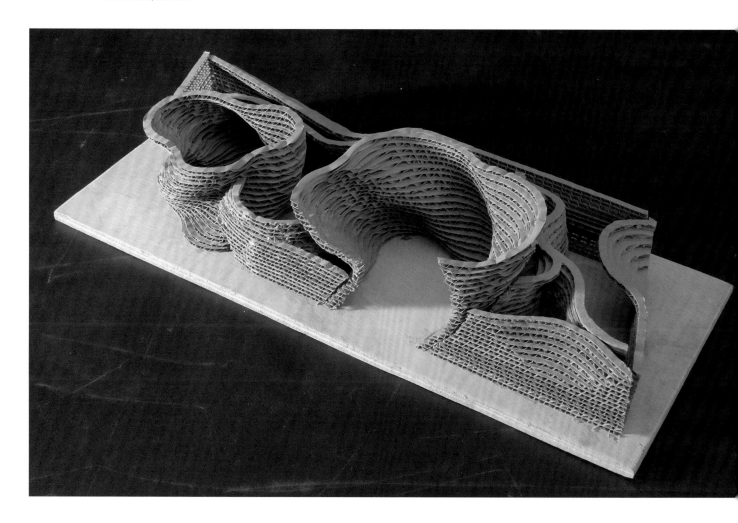

The engineering of a free form requires an open-minded approach in order to establish the archetypal structural system – or combination of systems – which best merges into its geometry; that is, which optimally exploits the potential structural advantages of its form.

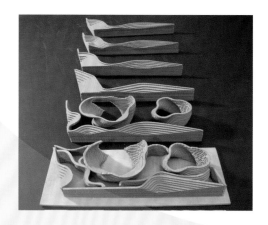

below: General
view prior to the
inauguration,
April 2010.

an adequate response to the loads. Thus the analogy of weaving also proved appropriate to the structuring of these global qualities.

The role of the computer software, both commercial and specifically developed for this project, was essential. The form was first devised as geometric NURBS (non-uniform rational B-splines) surfaces in Rhino software by the architecture team. After manipulating the form, the surfaces were cut by vertical and horizontal planes which resulted in curves that defined the axis of the corresponding structural tubes. This way, the double-curvature shape was formalised by the combination of two families – horizontal and vertical – of single-curvature tubes, reducing the complexity of the steel workshop manufacture. A further simplification for the production and manufacturing was the adaptation of the resulting variable curvature of the tubes to a reduced number of different curvatures which best fitted the geometry and were not discernible by the naked eye, as a departure from the ideal variable curvature.

From this 3-D geometric model generated by the architecture, the structural finite element method (FEM) model was developed, manipulated and analysed, giving feedback to the architectural team in an iterative process where the sizes, strengths and geometry of the different elements were adjusted according to strength and deformability criteria. For this purpose, specifically developed structural analysis software was used, enabling the fast importation

of the geometry from the CAD (Rhino) model, FEM non-linear analysis (ANSYS) and automatic post-processing of the results. This allowed the versatile procedure to reach an optimised solution that satisfied both the structural and architectural requirements.

The same geometrical model was later used by the steel workshop in the manufacture of all of the tubes, which required a precise geometry definition both at the workshop and during assembly on site. As a result, a unique geometric model served as the communication language between architectural design, structural analysis and workshop construction.

The engineering of a free form requires an open-minded approach in order to establish the archetypal structural system – or combination of systems – which best merges into its geometry; that is, which optimally exploits the potential structural advantages of its form. Finding the tensibility of a form is only possible through a deep understanding of its geometry and the inherent structural behaviour of its shape. The use of new computational software has now become such an enabling medium for this new synergy of complex design. △

Text © 2010 John Wiley & Sons Ltd. Images: pp 52-3, 56-8 © EMBT (Enric Miralles/
Benedetta Tagliabue; pp 54, 59 © Shen Zhonghai

Dominik Holzer
Steven Downing

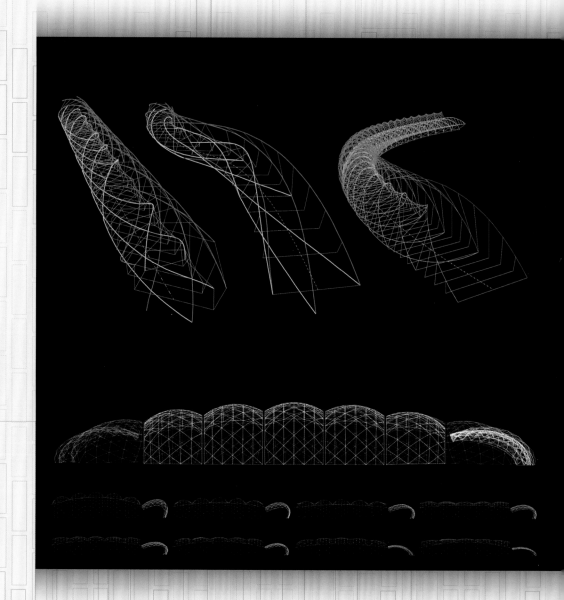

OPTIONEERING
A NEW BASIS FOR ENGAGEMENT BETWEEN ARCHITECTS AND THEIR COLLABORATORS

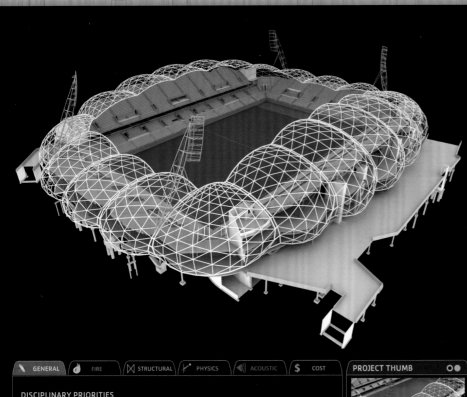

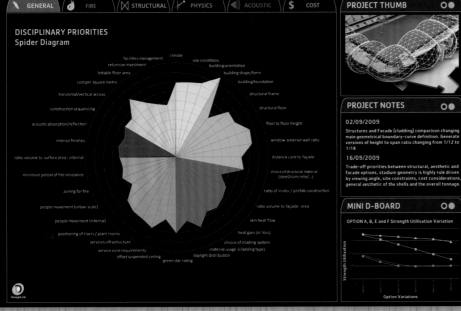

Conventionally, architects are somewhat tardy when inviting engineers to join their projects. By only introducing consulting engineers to participate in the later stages of the design process, engineers are commonly assigned a fixing role. This provides little opportunity for creative engineering solutions at the generative stage. Optioneering, a new business management model, however, offers the possibility of a new collaborative method for interaction between designers and their partners. **Dominik Holzer and Steven Downing** describe how a research project between the Spatial Information Research Laboratory (SIAL) at the Royal Melbourne Institute of Technology (RMIT) and the engineering firm Arup investigated the capability of this new form of collaboration.

Cox Architects, Arup and Architects 61,
Marina Bay Bridge, Singapore, 2006
opposite top: By creating a parametric model of the detailed steelwork, the modellers could begin work even though the critical bridge centreline was unknown. This centreline was sensitive to both the site geometry and design code requirements. Once the centreline was finalised, the parametric model was used in a one-off process to create geometry for structural analysis and a documentation model.

Cox Architects and Arup, Melbourne
Rectangular Stadium, Melbourne, 2007
opposite bottom: The steel roof consists of a series of connected diagrid shells. Together they form a complex system of load-bearing elements with highly irregular stress distribution in the individual members.

Dominik Holzer and Steven Downing,
Parametric variations of the Melbourne
Rectangular Stadium roof, Melbourne, 2006–07
top: Using a precursor of the tool-kit underlying the DesignLink computational framework, the structural design team was able to explore geometric design options without the laborious task of recreating structural analysis files for each geometry case/option. This allowed the team to evaluate and optimise more than 30 different design options in a one-week period, resulting in a significant reduction in the steelwork tonnage.

Dominik Holzer and Steven Downing, Mock-up of the DesignLink user interface, 2009
above: The DesignLink visual interface provides a common ground for simultaneous interpretation of performance indicators by practitioners from varying backgrounds. It helps to display the combined building performance impact the design team wants to look at for trade-offs and decision-making.

If investigating the traditional information flow between architects and their collaborators over the last century, one will mainly encounter a process in which architects ask their design partners to join a project at a certain stage to help them realise their ideas. Depending on the nature of collaboration and the type of disciplines involved, initial feedback from professional consultants often occurs too late – namely, at a time when many of the basic design drivers are already determined by the architect. In search of a more responsive approach to design, this article introduces a new method for interaction between designers and their consultants. 'Optioneering'.

Originating from business management practice in the mid-1990s,[1] optioneering is now making its way into architectural design of medium- and large-scale buildings. In a collaborative research project[2] between the Spatial Information Research Laboratory (SIAL) at the Royal Melbourne Institute of Technology (RMIT) and the engineering firm Arup, the possibilities of optioneering in everyday architectural and engineering context were investigated. During the three-year research project, strategies were developed for optioneering between collaborators at the outset of the design process. Flexible templates representing design intent allow the design team to compare and evaluate design options in regard to diverse performance criteria and to inform decision making in a complex, multi-criteria design environment.

Models, Methods and Tools in Computer-Integrated Collaborative Processes

Computationally assisted building analysis and simulation is revolutionising the work methods of architects and their collaborators. While in pre-digital times engineering analysis took days or even weeks to calculate, current tools allow consultants to back up design decisions much more quickly. This ever more concurrent response helps close the loop between morphological experimentation by architects and feedback from engineers. SIAL's research at Arup revealed that the increase in speed for information exchange requires architects and engineers to reconsider their collaborative planning and design methods. It also highlighted the benefits of starting collaboration on shared projects as early as possible.

In the practice-based research on live projects at Arup, two techniques have proven to be particularly useful in support of optioneering: parametric modelling and multi-criteria decision analysis (MCDA).

Parametric modelling tools helped the research team produce a quick turnaround of design options by allowing the generation of multiple design alternatives (called 'geometry cases') to keep a design in a flexible yet controlled state. By describing design geometry through 'recipes' rather than explicit values, aesthetic and engineering performance-based rules and criteria can be related across disciplinary boundaries.[3] Combined with suitable scripts for regenerating the analysis models based on changing geometry cases, this provided the freedom to truly explore design intent within predefined constraints, but without the typical time penalties associated with the generation and regeneration of analysis models.

One crucial aspect of operating successfully in the above context is the designers' facility for embedding key design parameters into the model via numerical input or 'logical' connections between dependent geometry. In this sense it is necessary to create a series of 'controls' to adjust and explore the design. In the case of the Marina Bay Bridge by Cox Architects, Arup and Architects 61 (Singapore, 2006), such controls helped to define the 'spine' of the bridge, while at the Melbourne Rectangular Stadium (Cox Architects and Arup, 2006–07) they regulated the span-to-depth ratio of the stadium roof and the curvature of individual shells. As with these two projects, the 2008 Beijing National Aquatics Center (Water Cube) by PTW Architects, Arup and China Construction Design International (CCDI) would have been impossible to realise without seamless and quick integration of geometric data between the architectural model, the analysis model and the documentation set.

At times during the search for optimised building performance, the point was reached where it was impossible to decide on the most appropriate among a larger set of solutions generated. Multi-criteria decision environments helped to evaluate complex problems where decisions can be subject to a high degree of uncertainty. Performance optimisation based on algorithms that help designers to solve complex multi-objective problems are common practice in other manufacturing industries such as ship-building and aerospace. Recent research shows how architects and engineers can profit form MCDA using 'Design of Experiments' (DoE).[4]

Flexible geometry templates that communicate design intent across disciplines and support automated MCDA processes for design evaluation provide collaborating teams with an array of possible design options. The SIAL research revealed that the increase of information generated in the context of optioneering needs to be complemented by a graphic user interface that allows for the appropriation and representation of design data across multiple disciplines. In order to facilitate such an interface, the DesignLink computational framework was developed at Arup.

Optioneering Through DesignLink

At certain times in the evolution of the design, it would be desirable for (all of these) parties to be looking at the same information (digital model and alphanumeric data) simultaneously, and moreover to be subsequently watching and commenting on the results of the various design modifications being made even as they happen.[5]

Optioneering encourages a form of discourse where design partners negotiate the criteria space for a design problem at the outset of their collaboration. DesignLink was designed to allow this to occur. Design partners can represent, analyse and trade off a rich array of performance criteria, thereby streamlining the decision-making process between architects and engineers. It provides multidisciplinary design teams with a common ground to reflect on the effects of each other's input. It does so by calling up applications, communicating between them and

Dominik Holzer, Diagram comparing
the traditional design process with the
optioneering method, 2009
One major aspect of optioneering is
the early collaboration of the design
team to quickly produce and analyse
multiple design options. The team then
makes informed decisions and trades
off priorities based on performance
feedback from multiple sources.

PTW Architects, Arup and China
Construction Design International
(CCDI), National Aquatics Center
(Water Cube), Beijing, 2008
Early collaboration between the
architects and engineers from many
disciplines resulted in a holistic
design concept, although only a
limited number of geometry options
were explored due to lack of suitable
parametric software. The use of
interoperability scripts enabled
the design team to significantly
increase the time available for
structural design and optimisation,
by decreasing the time required for
modelling and documentation.

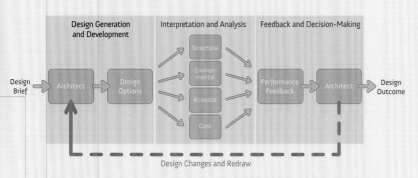

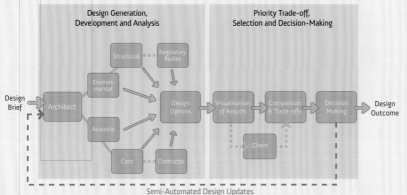

by storing design data for comparison and decision support. Using this framework, quantitative performance output responding to design alternatives are either published in custom views (structural/mechanical/environmental/facades/ etc), or compiled in a 'comparison' view. Results from different types of engineering (or even cost) analysis can thereby be juxtaposed in a visually explicit manner in one commonly accessible computational environment.

DesignLink is currently being tested and expanded at Arup and is being made freely available to collaborating industry partners.

Changing the Culture of Collaboration

Implementing the optioneering method will inevitably prompt architects to let go of the idea of being sole authors and to increasingly admit outside involvement from consultants. At the same time it requires consultants to step up as co-designers to become more proactively engaged in the design process. As a result, collaborators need to place stronger emphasis on defining the overarching design drivers and the performance parameters associated with them right at the beginning of a project.

Optioneering across architecture and engineering is still in its infancy. With increasing connectivity of project teams across professional boundaries we are likely to witness a vast array of challenging projects for which its application has become common practice in the not too distant future. ⌂

Notes
1. Encyclo, a UK-based online encyclopaedia, defines 'optioneering' as: 'a term increasingly used in industry when management needs to be confident of a course of action; particularly where regulatory or funding bodies seek a demonstration of due process.' See www.encyclo.co.uk/define/optioneering, accessed 15 February 2009.
2. The Delivering Digital Architecture in Australia Project was initiated by Professor Mark Burry from the Spatial Information Architecture Laboratory (SIAL) at RMIT University, Melbourne, and Richard Hough from Arup to investigate the impact of digital tools on architect/engineer collaboration.
3. In 2003, Andrew Maher and Professor Mark Burry (of SIAL) and Arup combined parametric design with engineering analysis for optimising the curvature of the Selfridges pedestrian bridge in Birmingham. See A Maher and MC Burry, 'The Parametric Bridge: Connecting digital design techniques in architecture and engineering', in Connecting – Crossroads of Digital Discourse (Proceedings of the 2003 Annual Conference of the Association for Computer Aided Design In Architecture), Indianapolis, 2003, pp 39–47. The research presented here also draws on the work of Kristina Shea and Maria Gourtovaial (University of Cambridge) and Robert Aish (Bentley Systems). Their combined use of the generative design tool eifForm with the associative modelling system Custom Objects (now Generative Components) allowed them to link performance optimisation with rule-based design. See K Shea, R Aish and M Gourtovaial, 'Towards integrated performance-driven generative design tools', in Digital Design (Proceedings of the 21st eCAADe conference), Graz, 2003, pp 103–10.
4. A detailed introduction to MCDA in an architectural and engineering design context can be found in Forest Flager, Ben Welle, Prasun Bansal, Grant Soremekun and John Haymaker, 'Multidisciplinary process integration and design optimization of a classroom building', ITcon, Vol 14, 2009, pp 595–612.
5. André Chaszar, 'Bridging the gap with collaborative design programs', Architectural Design, Vol 73, No 5, Wiley-Academy (London), 2003, pp 112–18.

Text © 2010 John Wiley & Sons Ltd. Images: p 60(t) © Arup, Cox, Architects 61, Singapore Urban Redevelopment Authority, image by Steven Downing; pp 60(b), 61(b), 63 © Dominik Holzer; p 61(t) © Arup – Jin Pae

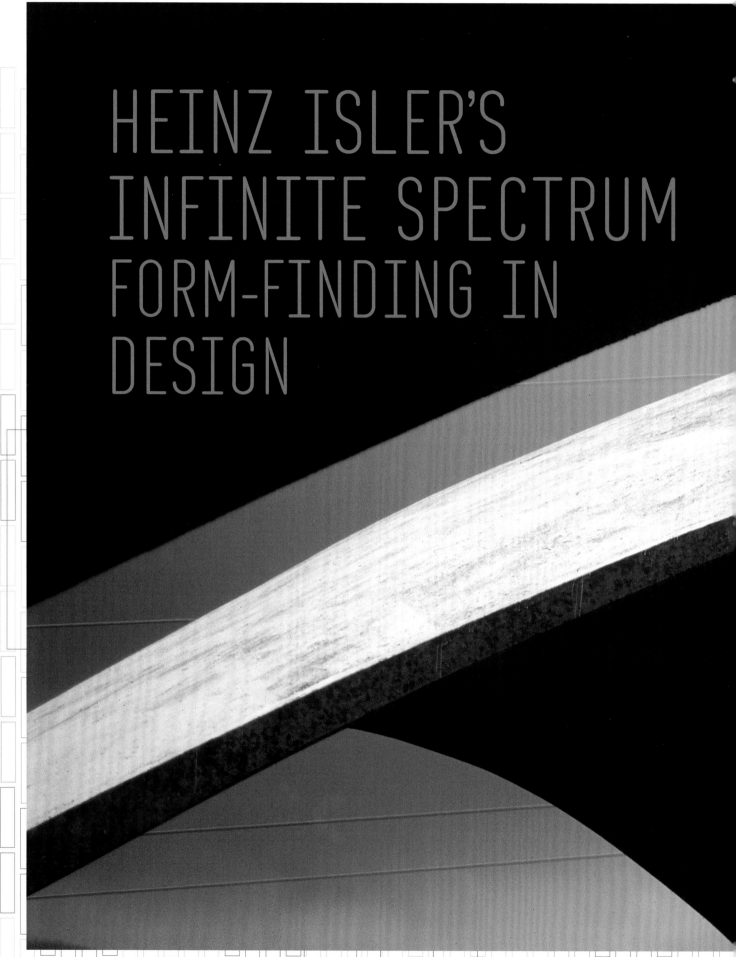

HEINZ ISLER'S INFINITE SPECTRUM FORM-FINDING IN DESIGN

Heinz Isler (1926–2009), the Swiss designer renowned for his shell structures, was extraordinary for his innovative and exacting work. He directly produced physical models by hand in order to not only create design prototypes, but also to generate scaled-up measurements for construction. **John Chilton** describes how Isler successfully applied the principle of the inverted catenary arch, which was first pioneered by Robert Hooke in Sir Christopher Wren's St Paul's Cathedral in the 17th century, to thin membrane structures in three dimensions.

Heinz Isler, Deitingen Süd Service Station, Flumenthal, Switzerland, 1968
These graceful synclastic forms are, for most of their area, just 90 millimetres (3.54 inches) thick and have no edge beams.

Heinz Isler
below: Heinz Isler
(1926–2009), designer
of innovative free-form
shells and structural artist,
photographed at his studio
in Lyssachschachen, near
Burgdorf, Switzerland, in
August 2003.

**Heinz Isler, 'Natural hills on
different edge lines', 1959**
right: Isler's own sketch of 39
'Natural hills on different edge
lines' in his paper 'New Shapes
for Shells' presented to the first
congress of the International
Association for Shell Structures
(IASS), in September 1959,
shows possible shapes for
shells and hints at the infinite
spectrum of further forms.

9 Natural hills on different edge lines.

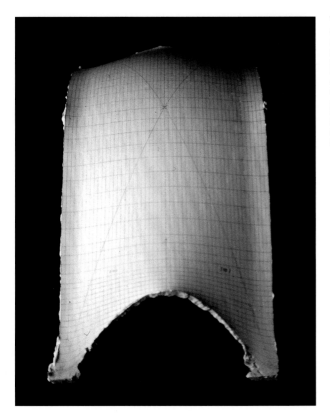

Heinz Isler, Precision measurement
left: Isler, always in person, took precise measurements of his physical models on a grid of points across the surface of the cast form, using a simple purpose-made jig. As can be seen here, he used a higher density of monitoring points in the more critical areas of greater curvature and near the supports.

Heinz Isler, Alternative models for a tennis hall shell
opposite bottom: To allow him to select the most appropriate form from the structural, economic and aesthetic point of view, Isler had to make multiple physical models for each application – here a series of trials for his tennis/sports halls, all of similar plan dimensions but with increasing rise.

When suspended between two supports under its own weight and the action of gravity, a flexible chain, cable or rope is subject only to tensile forces and forms a curve known as a catenary. Under the same load, this catenary, when inverted, is subject only to compression forces. The use of the inverted catenary to form an efficient arch was known as early as the late 17th and early 18th centuries. The British inventor, philosopher and architect Robert Hooke applied it in the 1670s when he was advising his friend Sir Christopher Wren on the rebuilding of St Paul's Cathedral. In 1748, it was used by Giovanni Poleni while he was investigating the appearance of cracks in the dome of St Peter's in Rome. Antoni Gaudí also used this principle in the structural design for the crypt of the Church of Colonia Güell, Santa Coloma de Cervelló, near Barcelona (1898–1914). However, the application of this principle to thin membranes in three dimensions was first successfully developed by the Swiss engineer Heinz Isler in the 1950s.

In the middle of the 20th century, recognised masters of reinforced concrete Eduardo Torroja, Félix Candela and Pier Luigi Nervi constructed shells more slender than traditional masonry domes and vaults. They based their forms on geometries easily describable by simple mathematical formulae. For instance, Torroja's Algeciras

Market Hall in Andalucia (1933) and Nervi's Palazzetto dello Sport, Rome (1957) were spherical dome segments, and Candela's Los Manantiales Restaurant in Mexico City (1957) was created from intersecting hyperbolic paraboloids. However, a paradigm shift occurred in September 1959 with the presentation, by Heinz Isler, of his paper 'New Shapes for Shells' at the first congress of the newly formed International Association for Shell Structures (IASS) in Madrid. In his brief paper, of approximately 50 lines of text and nine illustrations, Isler described three innovative methods for obtaining more complex and free-form surfaces: the freely shaped hill, the membrane under pressure and the hanging cloth reversed. He concluded with a page of hand-drawn sketches of 'Natural hills on different edge lines'; 39 in total, but with an 'etc' indicating the infinite spectrum available, commenting in the text that it gave 'a hint as to the tremendous variety of possible shell forms'.[1]

The impact of Isler's paper can be ascertained from the 300 lines of reported discussion, which included comments from Torroja, Ove Arup and Nicola Esquillan, the latter engineer for the then recently completed 206-metre (675.8-foot) span shell of the Centre of New Industries and Technologies (CNIT) in Paris. When closing this discussion

Isler is quoted as saying: 'So the engineer['s] problem is remaining all the same, but it is the first link, here, the shaping which has been lacking up to now, and this method can lead to a very nice solution. Thank you.'[2]

Isler's methods were based on physical modelling and experiment. For his inflated membranes and inverted hanging membranes, a plaster cast of the form was taken and accurately measured, always by him in person, in a purpose-made frame. This allowed precise coordinates to be taken for a grid of points over the surface. Following production of resin models, load-tested to prove structural adequacy, the measured dimensions were scaled up, suitable formwork was constructed and the shell cast – no computer-aided design (CAD), finite element analysis (FEA) or other computer systems were involved. In fact, to the end, the Isler office only ever had one computer and that was for word-processing!

The shells that led to Isler being described as a structural artist are primarily, but not exclusively, those derived from the hanging cloth reversed. Using this technique Isler created, for example, the elegant triangular shells of the Deitingen Süd Service Station (1968), the linked shells on seven supports for the Sicli factory in Geneva (1969), the outdoor theatres at Stetten and Grötzingen in collaboration with architect Michael Balz (1976–7), the hooded shells of the

Heinz Isler, Wyss Garden Centre, Solothurn, Switzerland, 1962
below left: The shell at the Wyss Garden Centre is based on an expansion form. Covering an area of 650 square metres (6,997 square feet), the main shell is just 70 millimetres (2.7 inches) thick and the stiffening edge cantilevers taper to just 60 millimetres (2.3 inches).

Heinz Isler, Bubble shells, Bösiger AG, Langenthal, Switzerland
bottom left: Hundreds of Isler 'bubble' shells were constructed, typically with spans of 20 x 20 metres (65.6 x 65.6 feet), mainly for industrial and commercial buildings, such as these for his preferred contractor Willi Bösiger AG of Langenthal, Switzerland, who continues to build the standard system. The largest bubble shell constructed, at Wangen bei Olten, measures 54.6 by 58.8 metres (179.1 x 192.9 feet).

Heinz Isler, Deitingen Süd Service Station, Flumenthal, Switzerland, 1968
below right: Isler's most iconic shells are the two triangular canopies, each 31.6 metres (103.6 feet) in span and up to 26 metres (85 feet) wide, constructed at Deitingen Süd Service Station, on the N1 highway between Zürich and Bern. Threatened with demolition in 1999, their retention was vigorously, and successfully, supported by Swiss architects including Mario Botta and Peter Zumthor.

Peter Rich Architects, Mapungubwe Interpretation Centre, Mapungubwe National Park, Limpopo, South Africa, 2008
bottom right: Isler's legacy of efficient compression forms lives on in projects such as the Mapungubwe Interpretation Centre which was selected as the World Architecture Festival's Building of the Year 2009. Here timbrel masonry vaults (by John Ochsendorf and Michael Ramage) of up to 14.5 metres (47.6 feet) in span and 300 millimetres (12 inches) thick, were constructed from unreinforced stabilised earth tiles, their form highly reminiscent of Isler's tennis halls.

Heinz Isler, Load-test model for shell of the Flieger Flab air museum, Dübendorf, near Zurich, 1987
left: Isler rigorously load-tested each new shell type using resin models monitored with strain gauges. The models were held in timber frames and loaded by a single weight hanging from an elaborate system of spreader beams and strings, as shown here for the 18.6 x 51.7 metre (61 x 169.6 foot) shells of an aircraft museum in collaboration with architects Haus + Herd.

Heinz Isler with Copeland Associates and Haus + Herd, Swimming pools, Norfolk Health & Racquets Club, Norwich, 1991
below: The wood-wool insulation used to line the formwork during construction is left in place, creating a warm and acoustically deadened environment for the swimming pools which typically span up to 35 x 35 metres (114.8 x 114.8 feet). The shell form elegantly reduces the heated volume while introducing natural daylight through the clear facades.

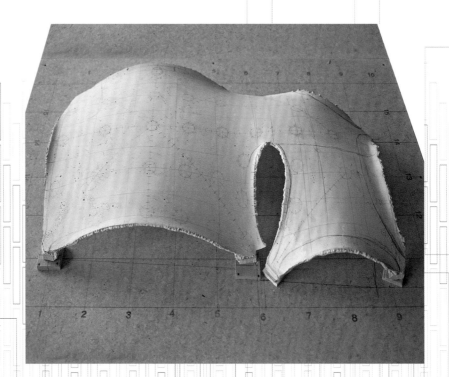

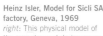

Heinz Isler, Model for Sicli SA factory, Geneva, 1969
right: This physical model of the complex and daring seven-point-supported double shell for the Sicli factory demonstrates Isler's method of form-finding. Possible edge lines for the shell, as built, can clearly be seen sketched on the surface of the cast. Here, at the request of the client and with the agreement of the architect, C Hilberer of Geneva, Isler was given complete control of the shell form.

Heinz Isler with Copeland
Associates and Haus + Herd,
Tennis halls, Norfolk Health &
Racquets Club, Norwich, UK, 1987
opposite bottom and right: Of Isler's
free-form shells derived from a hanging
membrane, the most common are
the swimming pool and tennis/sports
halls. The upturned edges provide
stiffening for the adjacent shells, which
spring directly from the ground. Due
to the quality of the concrete and
its permanent compressive state, no
waterproofing is required.

air museum at Dübendorf (1987) and his oft-repeated tennis hall and swimming pool shells.[3] It is unfortunate that, unlike the 'bubble' shells created using the inflated membrane method, which were used repeatedly for industrial shells of up to 55-metre (180.4-foot) spans, those generated from the hanging membrane were generally 'one-offs' or built in limited numbers due to the cost and complexity of the formwork. The exceptions were the tennis halls and swimming pools where clever adaptation allowed slightly different-sized shells to be cast using virtually the same formwork.

So why have Isler's methods not been copied? One reason may be because, although apparently simple, the processes are complex and require extreme precision – a trait that Isler had in profusion. This complexity is especially true for the hanging membranes, where he did not start with a flat plane between supports but deliberately chose a membrane surface of greater area with excess material at the perimeter, permitting initial sag. Consequently, there is, literally, an infinite number of alternatives and he needed to make and test sufficient examples to enable him to choose (or compromise) between the most economic in use of material, most structurally efficient and most aesthetically graceful. This was his skill as a designer and structural artist.

During conversations in March 2003, at the his studio in Lyssachschachen, with the author and Ekkehard Ramm, Isler reflected on what would happen to his unique approach to the form-finding of shells once he was gone – given that, at the time, his office employed just one person and he had no successor:

What is happening when I fall in the woods and I do not rise anymore? Then it is gone. No it's not gone ... the spiritual background of it (whether it be called the law, or the appreciation, or the understanding of the law) and the application of the law, that will go on. That is science. ... there are people who will be able to catch that, to understand that or to rediscover it in their own way.[4]

He was not wrong. For several years Mark West, from the University of Manitoba, inspired by Isler's work, has been using tensile membranes as formwork for efficient free-form structural elements as diverse as beams, columns, floor panels and cladding panels. More recently, although the construction material is different, the Mapungubwe Interpretation Centre in South Africa, by Peter Rich Architects, the World Architecture Festival's Building of the Year 2009, incorporates masonry vaults highly reminiscent of Isler's tennis halls. ⚙

Notes
1. Heinz Isler, 'New Shapes for Shells', Bulletin of the IASS, No 8, Paper C3, 1961.
2. Heinz Isler, Discussion (final paragraph): 'New Shapes for Shells', Bulletin of the IASS, op cit.
3. See John Chilton, *Heinz Isler*, Thomas Telford (London), 2000, pp 91–119.
4. Heinz Isler, recorded conversation with John Chilton and Ekkehard Ramm at Buro Isler, Lyssachschachen, near Burgdorf, Switzerland, 18 March 2003 (unpublished).

Text © 2010 John Wiley & Sons Ltd. Images: pp 64-5, 66(t&b), 67, 68(l&tr), 69-71© John Chilton; p 66(tr) © IASS Journal; p 68(br) © Peter Rich, photo Robert Rich

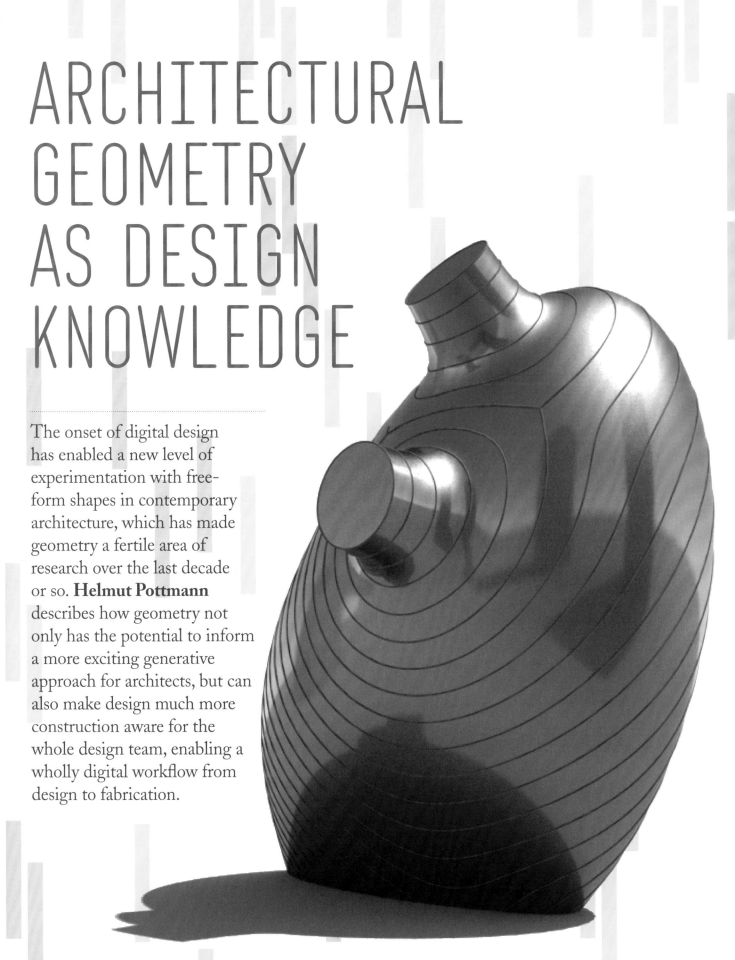

ARCHITECTURAL GEOMETRY AS DESIGN KNOWLEDGE

The onset of digital design has enabled a new level of experimentation with free-form shapes in contemporary architecture, which has made geometry a fertile area of research over the last decade or so. **Helmut Pottmann** describes how geometry not only has the potential to inform a more exciting generative approach for architects, but can also make design much more construction aware for the whole design team, enabling a wholly digital workflow from design to fabrication.

Helmut Pottmann

Formtexx, Skipper Library, conceptual design, 2009
This panellisation of the Skipper Library example issued by Formtexx is based on strips of nearly constant width and demonstrates how a non-regular connectivity of strips can be used to achieve this goal. It has been computed using Evolute's specially developed panellisation tool. Formtexx specialises in the manufacture of double-curvature free-form metal facades for the architectural sector (see www.formtexx.com).

Geometry has always constituted basic knowledge in the architectural design process, especially as a design language in the form of drawings based on the rules of descriptive geometry, but it has hardly ever formed an area of research. The advent of free-form shapes in contemporary architecture has completely changed this situation. The geometry of architectural designs is rapidly becoming more complex and challenging. Architects today exploit digital technology originally developed for the automotive and aeroplane industries for tasks of architectural design and construction.[1] This leads to a number of problems, since architectural applications differ from the original target industries in many ways, including aesthetics, statics and manufacturing technologies.

The advent of numerically controlled machining and other digital production technologies in the automotive and aviation industries has resulted in a significant body of research on appropriate mathematical representations and algorithmic solutions. Its main findings form the backbone of state-of-the-art 3-D modelling software. A similar development for architectural applications has just started; the resulting area of research may be called 'architectural geometry' (AG).[2]

Research in architectural geometry aims at the development of new tools for the creation of digital models for architecture which meet the requirements in the shape creation and design phase, and already incorporate basic aspects of the actual construction including materials, manufacturing technologies and structural properties. AG also plays an important role in enabling a completely digital workflow from design to manufacturing, especially for highly complex geometries. Moreover, it provides tools to transfer standard digital models into a form suitable for architectural application and fabrication – a process referred to as 'rationalisation'.

Construction-Aware Geometric Design vs Rationalisation
A construction-aware design approach incorporates knowledge of the material used, panel types, subconstruction and so on in the shape creation process via customised geometric modelling tools. As AG is not yet at the stage of design sophistication to deliver powerful software for accomplishing this approach, it is often necessary to enter a kind of redesign phase after the original geometry definition. This rationalisation has to recompute the geometry by minimally deviating from the original design and, at the same time, meeting requirements on panel types, smoothness of the skin, aesthetics of panel layout, cost of production and other aspects. From a mathematical perspective, rationalisation amounts to the solution of often highly non-linear and computationally expensive optimisation problems. The development of efficient optimisation algorithms and the incorporation into user-friendly rationalisation software tools are substantive research challenges in AG.

The methodology developed for rationalisation also opens up new avenues for the creation of novel construction-aware design tools. AG research has strong roots in applied mathematics, computational science and engineering, and can only meet its ambitious goals in close cooperation with architects, structural engineers and construction companies. These general claims and thoughts are illustrated in the selected research results and geometry consulting work of Evolute GmbH.[3]

The trend towards a high level of geometric complexity also has strong implications for geometry in architectural education. The effective use of powerful geometric design software already requires further knowledge of geometry than is traditionally taught in drawing or descriptive geometry courses, and an even deeper understanding is necessary to excel in the exploitation of parametric design technology.[4]

Architectural Free-Form Structures from Single-Curved Panels
Frank Gehry has been one of the first to employ free-form surfaces in architecture. Examples include the Guggenheim Museum in Bilbao (1997), the Experience Music Project in Seattle (2000) and the Walt Disney Concert Hall in Los Angeles (2004). The research performed in connection with his work is described in the PhD thesis of Dennis Shelden, Chief Technology Officer of Gehry Technologies.[5] This is also one of the first contributions to AG in the sense of the present article.

Gehry used mostly developable surfaces. These surfaces, also known as single-curved surfaces, can be unfolded into the plane without stretching or tearing. They are characterised by a family of straight lines, along each of which they possess a constant tangent plane. This implies various positive properties for fabrication. Recent research relates the coverage of a free-form surface by developable surface strips with work on quadrilateral meshes with planar faces.[6] A technique composed of subdivision (refinement) and optimisation towards developability provides a direct (construction-aware) modelling approach. The process of rationalisation of a given free-form surface with developable panels (strips) follows related ideas.

Rationalisation by Ruled Surfaces and Relation to Manufacturing Technologies
Ruled surfaces are formed by a family of straight lines and therefore possess advantages in fabrication. To give an example, ruled panels from glass-fibre-reinforced concrete can be produced more efficiently than general double-curved panels, since the rapid and inexpensive hot wire cutting technique can be used to manufacture their styrofoam moulds. Generically, ruled surfaces possess negative Gaussian curvature (K), which means that they are locally saddle shaped; they may also be single-curved ($K=0$). Hence designs which contain large areas with non-positive K are promising candidates for rationalisation with ruled panels. Software for performing this task has recently been developed by Evolute. An example of its application is Zaha Hadid's Cagliari Contemporary Arts Centre in Sardinia (2007).

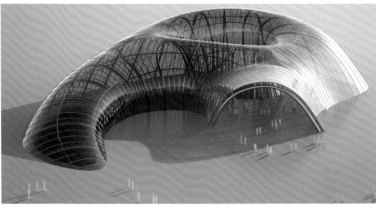

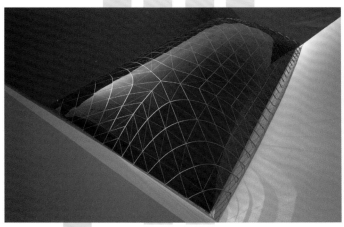

top and centre: Combining subdivision and optimisation (centre) provides construction-aware geometric design, a direct approach to modelling free-form surfaces which are composed of single-curved strips. A result of this technique is shown in the two views (top) of an experimental case study.

above: Ongoing research by Evolute and RFR Engineers, Paris, aims at the combined treatment of geometry, structure and manufacturing. This is illustrated here by the example of a shell acting as a roof of a courtyard with a rectangular base. The shell's shape and its rationalisation into single-curved or, more precisely, cylindrical panels were found by means of structural form-finding combined with geometric optimisation.

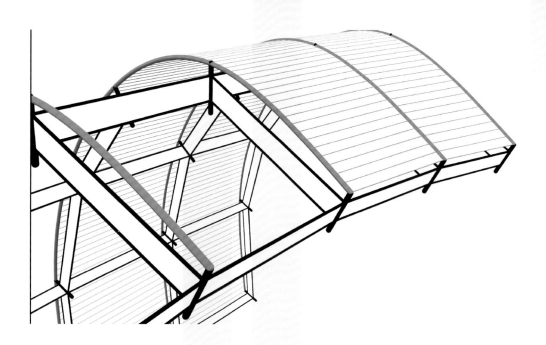

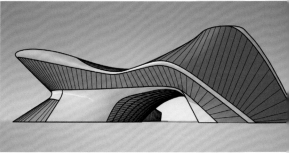

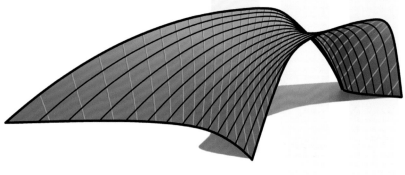

top: The close relationship between the coverage of a surface by single-curved strips and quadrilateral meshes with planar faces leads to the development of supporting structures with straight beams and well-defined node axes for single-curved panel arrangements on free-form shapes. This technology couples geometry and construction (patent pending).

Zaha Hadid Architects, Contemporary Arts Centre, Cagliari, Sardinia, 2007
above: This design contains large areas which can be covered by ruled surfaces (upper right), whereas more complicated saddle-shaped parts may be rationalised by a smooth union of ruled strips (bottom left). The asymptotic curves (curves with vanishing normal curvature) depicted lower right are partially nearly straight and thus indicate the potential for rationalisation with ruled surfaces. The algorithmic techniques employed in this rationalisation study by Evolute are linked to manufacturing geometry (CNC machining) and hot wire cutting of moulds.

opposite: On this surface, three curve families which are close to geodesics (shortest paths) are arranged in a trihexagonal pattern. Geodesic curve families are preferred for cladding with wooden planks. The trihex arrangement of three such families is especially useful for the construction of timber grid-shells. The computation of this example (by Evolute) is based on the same mathematical representation and optimisation principle as that for the Skipper Library example. So far, this is the pure result of AG, but future research will aim at combining geometric and structural optimisation.

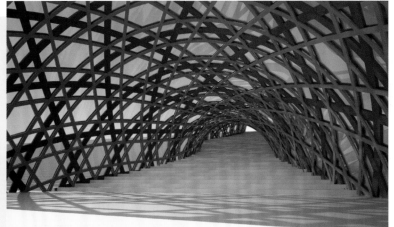
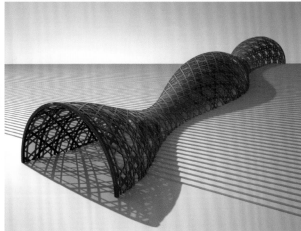

Panel Layout

Recent developments in manufacturing technology for double-curved metal panels suggest that large-scale free-form metal facades will be buildable in the near future. This technological advancement will eventually simplify the rationalisation of a metal facade surface, but splitting the surface into panels of maximum manufacturable size is still required. State-of-the-art design tools do not yet efficiently support the design of such panel layouts for complex free-form surfaces. In the paradigm of parametric modelling, this often leads to free-form surfaces being replaced by simple parametric surfaces at an early stage. Recent research therefore tries to close these gaps, treating arbitrary free-form surfaces as parameters themselves and fully parametrising their panel layouts.

Future Research

Architectural geometry constitutes a new and challenging research area which aims at providing construction-aware design tools and enabling a completely digital workflow from design to manufacturing, especially for highly complex geometries. While complex geometry mostly in relation to surfaces has been illustrated here, future research must also address fully spatial structures. The tools which are currently being developed have some built-in detail knowledge of AG, but their efficient use requires a solid understanding of geometry which goes beyond the content of the traditional geometry curriculum in architecture. Future academic developments will need to address these new challenges in order to recognise the emerging significance of geometry as architectural knowledge. ᴆ

Notes

1. CATIA is one of the first and most prominent examples of software transferred from the automotive and aircraft industries into architecture, namely by Frank Gehry. NURBS-based modellers, such as Rhino, are mainly based on technologies originally developed for applications other than architecture.
2. See Helmut Pottmann, Michael Hofer and Axel Kilian (eds), *Advances in Architectural Geometry*, Vienna, 2008; see www.architecturalgeometry.at/aag08.
3. Evolute GmbH is a spin-off from Helmut Pottmann's research group at TU Vienna, which performs research, development and consulting in geometric computing for architecture and manufacturing technologies; see www.evolute.at
4. See Helmut Pottmann, A Asperl, M Hofer and A Kilian, *Architectural Geometry*, Bentley Institute Press (Exton, PA), 2007, which provides support for meeting the resulting challenges in education and also leads the way from basic high-school geometry to research in AG.
5. Dennis Shelden, 'Digital surface representation and the constructability of Gehry's architecture', PhD thesis, MIT, 2002.
6. See Helmut Pottmann, Alexander Schiftner, Pengbo Bo, Heinz Schmiedhofer, Wenping Wang, Niccolo Baldassini and Johannes Wallner, 'Freeform surfaces from single curved panels', *ACM Transactions on Graphics 27*, 2008. Ongoing related research is funded via Project 230520 of the FP7-IAPP framework; project partners TU Wien, Evolute and RFR Engineers, Paris (www.rfr.fr).

Text © 2010 John Wiley & Sons Ltd. Images: pp 72-3 © Image courtesy of Alexander Schiftner, Heinz Schmiedhofer and Formtexx; p 75(t&c) © Images courtesy of Alexander Schiftner, Pengbo Bo, Johannes Wallner and Heinz Schmiedhofer; p 75(b) Images courtesy of RFR; p 76(t) Image courtesy of Alexander Schiftner; p 76(b) Upper left image courtesy of Zaha Hadid Architects, other images courtesy of Simon Flöry and Heinz Schmiedhofer; p 77 © Image courtesy of Alexander Schiftner, Johannes Wallner and Heinz Schmiedhofer

Neri Oxman

STRUCTURING MATERIALITY

DESIGN FABRICATION OF HETEROGENEOUS MATERIALS

What happens when we invert the usual sequence of the design process – form–structure–material – so materiality becomes the generative driver? Taking nature as her model, **Neri Oxman** advocates a new material method, Variable Property Design (VPD), in which material assemblies are modelled, simulated and fabricated with varying properties in order to correspond with multiple and continuously shifting functional constraints.

**Neri Oxman, Beast: Prototype for a Chaise Longue,
Museum of Science, Boston, Massachusetts, 2009**
The chaise combines structural, environmental and
corporeal performance by adapting its thickness, pattern
density, stiffness, flexibility and translucency to load,
curvature and skin-pressured areas respectively. It is
patterned with five different materials color-coded by elastic
moduli. Stiff and soft materials are distributed according to
the user's structural load distribution; soft silicon 'bumps'
are located in regions of higher pressure.

Neri Oxman, Beast: Prototype for a Chaise Longue,
Museum of Science, Boston, Massachusetts, 2009
opposite left (Bottom): Detail of 3-D physical construction
and material weighing charts. Stiffer materials (distributed
in vertical regions under compression) are dark while softer
materials (distributed in horizontal regions under tension)
are translucent. (Top): Material weighing chart. The elastic-
modulus of each component is defined relative to its stress,
strain and comfort profile. An algorithm then assigns one out
of five materials for physical construction.

Neri Oxman, Monocoque: Prototype for a
Structural Skin, Museum of Modern Art
(MoMA), New York, 2007
opposite right: Monocoque illustrates a
process for stiffness distribution informed
by structural load based on a Voronoi
algorithm. The distribution of shear-stress
lines and surface pressure is embodied
in the allocation and relative thickness of
the stiff vein-like elements built into the
skin (black) and the soft (white) cellular
components between them.

*In her [nature's] inventions
nothing is lacking, and
nothing is superfluous.*
Leonardo da Vinci

Nature is demonstrably sustainable. Its challenges have been resolved over eons with enduring solutions with maximal performance using minimal resources. Unsurprisingly, nature's inventions have for all time prompted human achievements and have led to the creation of exceedingly effective materials and structures, as well as methods, tools, mechanisms and systems by which to design them.

Structuring Difference: Nature's Way
Natural structures possess the highest level of seamless integration and precision with which they serve their functions. A key distinguishing trait of nature's designs is its capability in the biological world to generate complex structures of organic or inorganic multifunctional composites such as shells, pearls, corals, bones, teeth, wood, silk, horn, collagen and muscle fibres.[1] Combined with extracellular matrices, these structural biomaterials form microstructures engineered to adapt to prearranged external constraints introduced upon them during growth and/or throughout their life span.[2] Such constraints generally include combinations of structural, environmental and corporeal performance. Since all biological materials are made of fibres, their multifunctionality often occurs at scales that are nano through macro and typically achieved by mapping performance requirements to strategies of material structuring and allocation. The shape of matter is therefore directly linked to the influences of force acting upon it.[3] Material is concentrated in regions of high strength and dispersed in areas where stiffness is not required. It is a well-known fact that in nature, shape is cheaper than material, yet material is cheap because it is effectively shaped and efficiently structured.

Nature's ability to distribute material properties by way of locally optimising regions of varied external requirements, such as bone's ability to remodel under altering mechanical loads, or wood's capacity to modify its shape by way of containing moisture, is facilitated, fundamentally, by its ability to simultaneously model, simulate and fabricate material structuring. The structural properties of wood, for instance, not unlike most biological materials, can widely vary when measured with the growth grain or against it, such that its

hardness and strength may differ for a given sample when measured in different orientations. This property is called 'anisotropy', and it is due to 'anisotropic structuring' that nature can create sustainable structures efficiently.

From Discrete to Continuous Heterogeneous Material Architectures
Compared to nature, our own material strategies appear to be much less effective, and mostly wasteful. Since the industrialised age, the construction industry has been dependent on discrete solutions for distinct functions.[4] Building skins are a great example of such a claim. Steel and glass possess significantly different structural and environmental properties which relate to significantly different performance requirements. Diversity is achieved by sizing rather than by substance variation, and it is typically mass-produced, not customised. As far as material structuring is considered, in the artificial world, especially in the construction industry, one property fits all. Can nature's ability be emulated in the design of the artificial?

Form First, Structure First, Material First: New Materialism
The image of the architect as form-giver has for centuries dominated the profession. In most cases, structural strategies are addressed by way of post-rationalisation in support of the building's utility captured by spatial properties. In this light, material selection and application are dependent on structural solutions. Such views emphasise the hierarchical nature of the design process with form being the first article of production, driving both structural and material strategies. Frank Gehry's architecture provides many such examples; parallel to a 'form first' approach and influenced by the work ethic of leading structural engineers such as Arup and Buro Happold, an alternative schema prioritises the function of structure as the main driver of formal expression.

'Structure first' is manifested particularly in projects of engineering complexity such as bridges and skyscrapers. Conversely, material has traditionally been regarded as a feature of form, but not its originator. In nature, it appears, the hierarchical sequence 'form–structure–material' is inverted

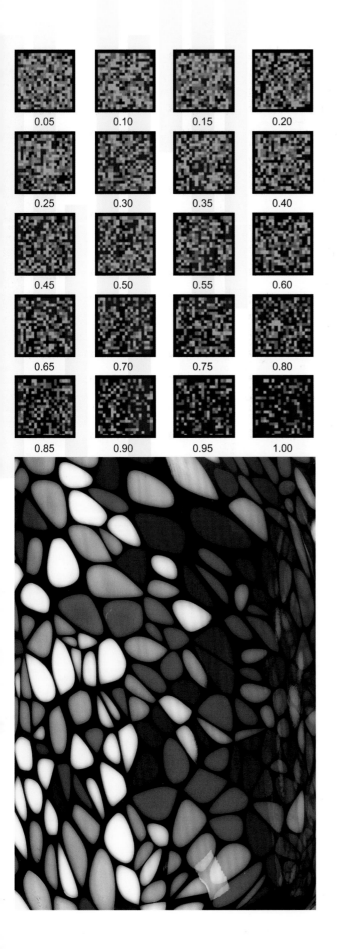

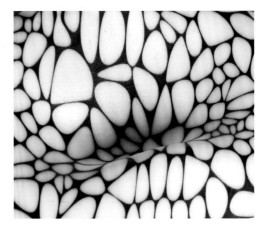

bottom-up as material informs structure which, in turn, informs the shape of naturally designed specimens. Such is the case, for instance, with bones and other cellular structures, the shape of which is directly informed by the materials from which they are made. In nature, in most cases, material comes first. How can a 'material first' approach be accommodated by design?

With the assistance of advances in structural and material engineering entering contemporary discourse, architectural culture appears poised for transformation. Designers now seek to advance nature's strategies in structuring matter by designing synthetic multifunctional materials competing with evolution's unrestricted time frame of design process. Fitness, not form, is what actually matters. Welcome the new materiality.

The New Materiality: Defining a Novel Technology of Variable Property Design Fabrication

Variable property design (VPD) is a design approach, a methodology and a technical framework by which to model, simulate and fabricate material assemblies with varying properties designed to correspond to multiple and continuously varied functional constraints. Such capability is here termed 'synthetic anisotropy' – an ability to strategically control the density and directionality of material substance in the generation of form. In this approach, material precedes shape, and it is the structuring of material properties as a function of performance that anticipates their form. Theoretical and technical foundations for this approach have been termed 'material-based design computation'.[5]

The mechanical response of materials designed and engineered with spatial gradients in composition and structure appears to be of considerable significance in all subdisciplines of design – from product design, to medical devices, to buildings as well as technologies to fabricate and construct them. The following projects illustrate an array of implementations for this approach in the design of a furniture product, a medical device and a fabrication technology. All projects integrate the components of modelling, analysis and fabrication with a particular focus on the development of one such component in each of the projects.

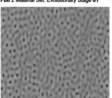
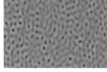

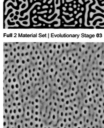
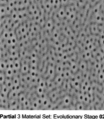
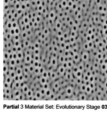
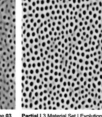

Full 2 Material Set: Evolutionary Stage **01** **Full** 2 Material Set: Evolutionary Stage **02** **Full** 2 Material Set | Evolutionary Stage **03** **Full** | 2 Material Set | Evolutionary Stage **04**

Partial 3 Material Set: Evolutionary Stage **01** **Partial** 3 Material Set: Evolutionary Stage **02** **Partial** 3 Material Set: Evolutionary Stage **03** **Partial** | 3 Material Set | Evolutionary Stage **04**

Neri Oxman, Carpal Skin: Prototype for a Carpel
Tunnel Syndrome Splint, Museum of Science,
Boston, Massachusetts, 2009
left: Physical model of prototype. Material
distribution charts illustrating a range of potential
solutions informed by size, scale, direction and
ratio between soft and stiff materials. The charts
are computed on top of an optimised unfolded
representation of the frontal and dorsal planes of
the patient's hand and refolded following material
assignment to construct the 3-D glove.

opposite bottom: Detail illustrating the distribution of material properties as a function of movement constraint and control. The custom-fit property-distribution functions built into the glove allow for passive yet consistent pulling and stretching simultaneously.

below left: Digital model of prototype. Local thickness changes correspond to strategic areas across the surface area of the wrist in cushioning and protecting it from hard surfaces as well as allowing for a comfortable grip. These thickened bumps also increase flexibility, enhance circulation and relieve pressure on the median nerve as it acts as a soft tissue-reshaping mechanism.

below right: Physical model of prototype. In this particular prototype, stiff materials constrain the lateral bending motion at the wrist, and can be identified by the oblique trajectory of dark and stiff materials. Soft materials allow for ergonomic wrist support and comfort through movement.

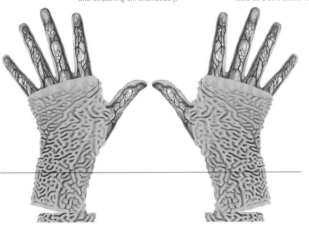
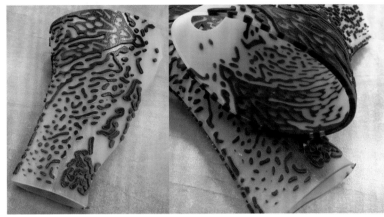

Variable Property Modelling (VPM): Prototype for a Chaise Longue, Museum of Science, Boston, Massachusetts, 2009

A single continuous surface acting both as structure and skin is locally modulated to provide for both support and comfort. This design for a chaise longue corresponds to structural, environmental and corporeal performance by adapting its thickness, pattern density and stiffness to load, curvature and skin-pressured areas respectively. The technical objective was to introduce a quantitative characterisation and analysis of VPM as it is applied to a tiling algorithm using Voronoi cell tessellation.[6] Stiffer materials are positioned in surface areas under compression, and softer, more flexible materials in surface areas under tension.[7]

Variable Property Analysis (VPA): Carpal Skin: Prototype for a Carpel Tunnel Syndrome Splint, Museum of Science, Boston, Massachusetts, 2009

Similar to the manner by which load or temperature can be plotted and computationally optimised to fit their function, physical pain may also be mapped in the design and production of medical assistive devices such as pain-reducing splints. Carpal Skin is a prototype for a treatment glove for carpal tunnel syndrome. The syndrome is a medical condition in which the median nerve is compressed at the wrist, leading to numbness, muscle atrophy and weakness in the hand. Night-time wrist splinting is the recommended treatment for most patients before going into carpal tunnel release surgery. The main problem with current glove solutions is their lack of customised features in relation to the patient's distribution of pain. Carpal Skin is a process by which to map the pain profile of a particular patient – intensity and duration – and distribute hard and soft materials corresponding to the patient's anatomical and physiological requirements. The relative distribution of softer and stiffer materials across the glove's surface area allows limiting central and lateral bending motions locally in a highly customised fashion.

Variable Property Fabrication (VPF)

Currently, there exists no rapid prototyping technology that allows for a continuous modification of material properties such as strength, stiffness, density and elasticity as continuous gradients across the surface and volume area of a functional component. Such variations are usually achieved as discrete changes in physical behaviour by printing multiple components with different properties and distinct delineations between materials, and assembling them only after the fabrication process has been completed. Such processes result in material waste and lack of functional precision. Variable property fabrication aims at introducing a novel material deposition 3-D printing technology[8] which offers gradation control of multiple materials within one print to save weight and material quantity while reducing energy inputs. The result is a continuous gradient material structure, highly optimised to fit its structural performance with an efficient use of materials, reduction of waste and the production of highly customised features with added functionality.

Materials are the New Software

Since its emergence in the 1960s, computer-aided design (CAD) in its many transformations has afforded the designer an almost effortless manipulation of shapes generally detached from their fabrication in material form. Such processes promote the application of material subsequent to the generation of form. Even when supported by high-fidelity analytical tools for analysis and optimisation, these processes are predominantly linked to geometrical manipulations in three dimensions. The work presented here calls for a shift from a geometric-centric to a material-based approach in computationally enabled form-generation.

Variable property fabrication of materials with heterogeneous properties across a wide array of scales and applications holds a profound place in the future of

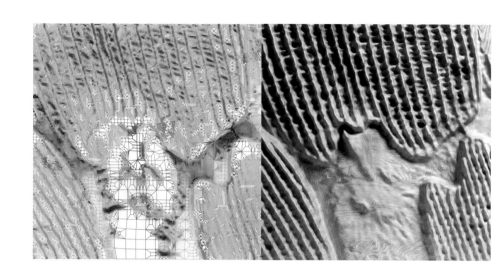

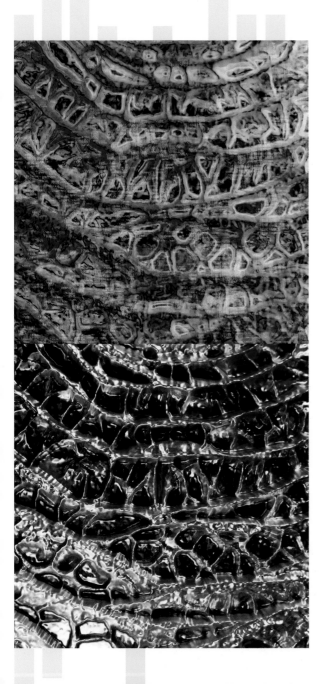

Neri Oxman, Raycounting, Museum of
Modern Art (MoMA), New York, 2007
opposite bottom: Raycounting is a method
for originating form by registering the
intensity and orientation of light rays.
3-D surfaces of double curvature are the
result of assigning light parameters to
flat planes. The algorithm calculates the
intensity, position and direction of one, or
multiple, light sources placed in a given
environment and assigns local curvature
and material stiffness values to each point
in space corresponding to the reference
plane, the light dimension and structural
stability requirements.

Neri Oxman, Subterrain: Variable
Property Analysis and Fabrication of a
Butterfly Wing, Museum of Modern Art
(MoMA), New York, 2007
opposite top: An object-oriented application
determines the material's behaviour
according to stress, strain, heat flow, stored
energy and deformation due to applied loads
and temperature differences. The tissue is
reconstructed using a CNC mill and wood
composites. In this case fibre directionality
assignment and layering strategies are
employed for areas requiring structural
stiffness as defined by the designer.

Neri Oxman, [X, Y, Z, S, S, T]
(pronounced 'exist'): Variable
Property Analysis and Fabrication of
Natural Specimens, 2008
below: Aluminium and low carbon
steel composite. The 6-D model
includes 2-D information (X, Y), out of
plane deformation (Y), elastic stress
(S), strain (S) and temperature flux
(T). The tissue is reconstructed using a
CNC mill and metal/steel composites.
In this case material layering strategies
are employed for areas requiring
structural stiffness as defined by the
designer.

design and engineering. The ability to synthetically
engineer and fabricate such materials using VPF
strategies appears to be incredibly promising as it
increases the product's structural and environmental
performance, enhances material efficiency, promotes
material economy and optimises material distribution.
Among other contributions, material-based design
computation promotes a design approach through
digital fabrication of heterogeneous materials
customised to fit their structural and environmental
functions. The practice of architecture is at last
reawakening to its new role as (a) second nature. ∆

Notes

1. Janine M Benyus, *Biomimicry: Innovation Inspired by Nature*,
HarperCollins Publishers Inc (New York), 1997.
2. Julian Vincent, *Structural Biomaterials*, Princeton University
Press (Princeton, NJ), 1982.
3. Steven Vogel, *Comparative Biomechanics: Life's Physical
World*, Princeton University Press (Princeton, NJ), 2003.
4. Neri Oxman, 'Oublier Domino: On the evolution of architectural
theory from spatial to performance-based programming', First
International Conference on Critical Digital: What Matters(s)?,
Harvard University Graduate School of Design (Cambridge, MA),
18–19 April 2008, pp 393–402.
5. Some relevant foundations of material-based design computation
appear in: Neri Oxman and JL Rosenberg, 'Material-based
design computation: an inquiry into digital simulation of physical
material properties as design generators', *International Journal of
Architectural Computing* (IJAC), Vol 5, No 1, 2007, pp 26–44;
Neri Oxman, 'Get real: towards performance-driven computational
geometry', *International Journal of Architectural Computing*, Vol 5,
No 4, 2007, pp 663–84; Neri Oxman, 'FAB finding: predicting the
future', *Proceedings of the 25th eCAADe Conference*, Frankfurt am
Main, 26–29 September 2007, pp 785–92.
6. Neri Oxman, 'Material-based design computation: Tiling
behavior', reForm: Building a Better Tomorrow, Proceedings of the
29th Annual Conference of the Association for Computer Aided
Design in Architecture, Chicago, 22–25 October 2009, pp 122–9.
7. Material and mathematical studies were carried out in
collaboration with Professor Craig Carter and Professor Lorna
Gibson from the Department of Materials Science and Engineering
at MIT.
8. 2010, MIT patent pending.

Text © 2010 John Wiley & Sons Ltd. Images © Neri Oxman, Architect and
Designer

Fabian Scheurer

MATERIALISING COMPLEXITY

The specialist practice designtoproduction consults on the digital production of complex architectural designs. Here, co-founder **Fabian Scheurer** charts the relatively recent journey that architecture has taken from the regular to the irregular. He provides a comprehensive account of how this shift to curvilinear and complex forms has impacted on design and production methods, and the strengths and pitfalls of parametric design and CNC fabrication.

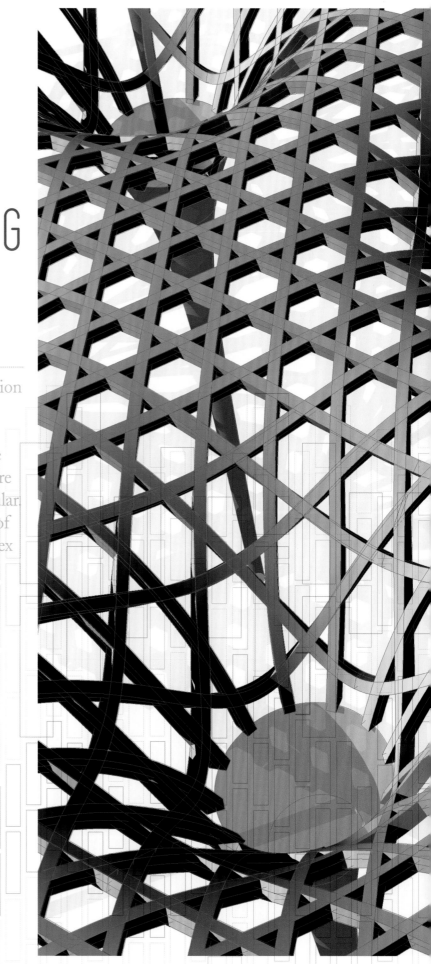

Shigeru Ban, Nine Bridges Golf Resort, Yeoju, South Korea, 2009

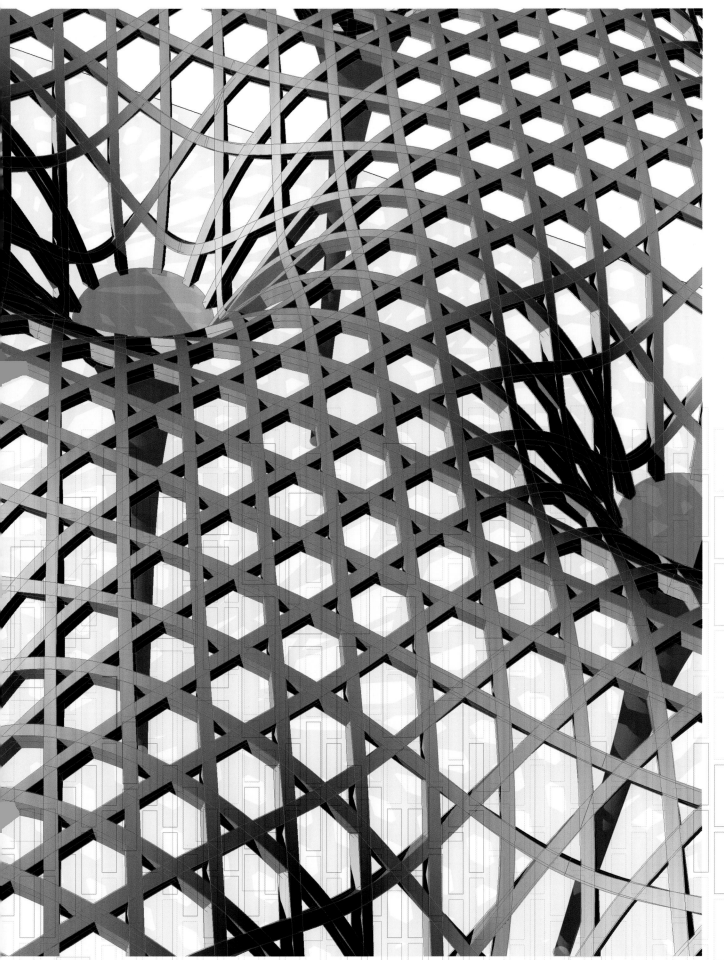

Designers, especially well prepared to deal
with ambiguous, ill-defined problems,
suddenly had to come up with unambiguous,
well-defined, formal descriptions,
syntactically correct to the last semicolon.

**Zaha Hadid Architects, Hungerburgbahn,
Innsbruck, Austria, 2007**
top left: The four new stations designed by Zaha
Hadid for the Hungerburg funicular contain more
than 2,500 unique custom-cut polyethylene
profiles that connect the glass cladding of the
roof to the steel ribs of the supporting structure.
designtoproduction implemented an automated
workflow for detailing and fabrication planning of
the profiles. The process started with a CAD model
provided by the engineers and ended with delivering
machine-ready manufacturing data directly to the
five-axis CNC router that cut the profiles.

**Renzo Piano Building Workshop, Peek &
Cloppenburg Weltstadhaus, Cologne, 2005**
top right: The facade of the department
store is covered with 6,500 glass panels
mounted in delicate wooden girders. To
meet the budgetary requirements, the
double-curved surface was assembled from
flat quadrilateral panels. designtoproduction
conceived a parametric model of the facade
and optimised the horizontal and vertical
panel segmentation so that the distance
between the edges of the planar panels could
be absorbed by the framing.

SANAA, EPFL Rolex Learning Center, Lausanne, 2010
above and opposite: The large, double-curved concrete
slab of SANAA's learning centre required a specific
formwork solution. A smoothly curved surface of 7,500
square metres (80,731 square feet) was constructed
in combination with standard scaffolding components,
using nearly 1,500 individual wooden boxes.
designtoproduction automated the planning process,
starting with a 3-D model of the slab surface, and
resulting in detailed plans for all of the 1,500 formwork
tables and the machine data for the CNC cutting of
almost 10,000 individual cleats.

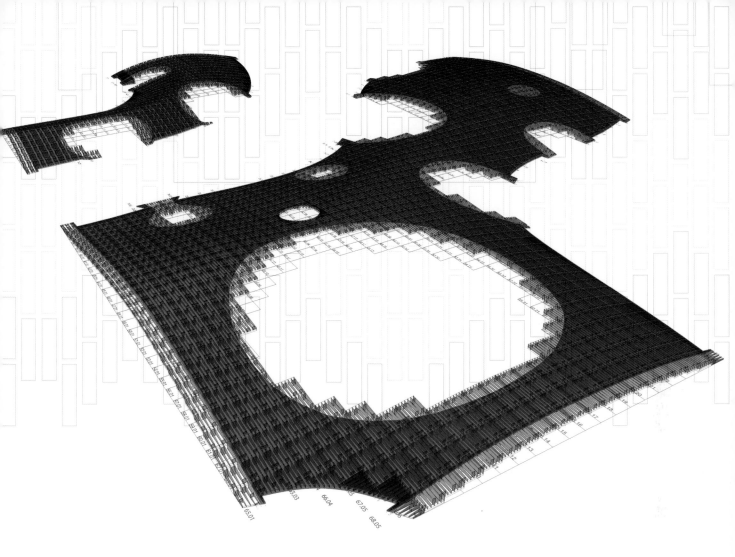

Since it was founded in 2006, designtoproduction has been searching for a single term that explains the central core of its services to architects, engineers and fabricators. But even branding experts have not been able to boil the lengthy explanations down to a single sentence. Despite this marketing void, the firm's enterprise has been solidly successful. Obviously, a niche has opened up in the building workflow that lacks a name but is nevertheless full of opportunities. Where did it come from? Let us speculate.

Regular to Non-Regular

By the mid-1990s an innovation had finally found its way from the French car industry into the CAD software used by designers. Splines and non-uniform rational B-spline surfaces (NURBS) developed at the laboratories of Renault and Citroën as mathematical definitions for curves and curved surfaces in the 1950s, suddenly appeared in the program menus of designing architects. And apparently they liked it.

The curvy, non-orthogonal, non-regular, 'blobby' results can be visited all over the world. But it quickly became apparent that these designs would pose completely new challenges once they had been sold to a sufficiently funded client and entered the construction design and building phase. What had started as a happy trip away from repetitive, industrialised, orthogonal boredom became a labour-intensive nightmare. Suddenly, facade panels had to be curved, like on the roofs of Zaha Hadid's (2007) Hungerburg funicular stations in Innsbruck, Austria (expensive). Or the panellisation had to be meticulously optimised to approximate the curves with planar facets, like on Renzo Piano's (2005) Peek & Cloppenburg department store in Cologne (difficult). And where the panels met, no longer were there repeating details that could be drawn once and multiplied over a whole building. Thanks to the non-regular shape, every panel and every joint had a slightly different geometry. The convenient set of standard detail drawings was replaced by hundreds and thousands of individual workshop drawings.

Concrete to Abstract

Fortunately, some CAD systems at that time – just a few years ago – had programming interfaces (APIs) that allowed one to 'remote control' the drawing tools from an algorithm. Smart, but lazy, architects, like designtoproduction partner Arnold Walz, immediately seized the opportunity and started to program drawing algorithms instead of drawing countless variants of the same thing by hand (or mouse). Such an algorithm takes the defining properties of a component or joint as input parameters and delivers a perfect drawing or 3-D model as output. The information of a thousand drawings can thus be reduced into one well-defined algorithm and a thousand small sets of only a few parameters. But again, this trick posed new challenges. First, you need to know how to program. Designers, especially well prepared to deal with ambiguous, ill-defined problems, suddenly had to come up with unambiguous, well-defined, formal descriptions, syntactically correct to the last semicolon. Second, you need to abstract the problem. Finding an elegant, common

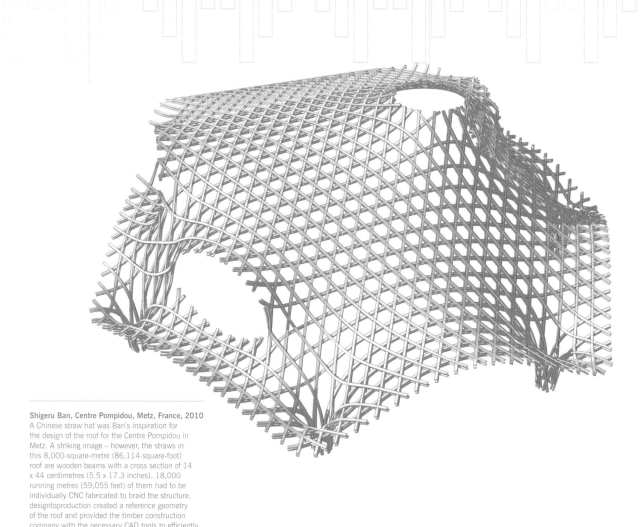

Shigeru Ban, Centre Pompidou, Metz, France, 2010
A Chinese straw hat was Ban's inspiration for
the design of the roof for the Centre Pompidou in
Metz. A striking image – however, the straws in
this 8,000-square-metre (86,114-square-foot)
roof are wooden beams with a cross section of 14
x 44 centimetres (5.5 x 17.3 inches). 18,000
running metres (59,055 feet) of them had to be
individually CNC fabricated to braid the structure.
designtoproduction created a reference geometry
of the roof and provided the timber construction
company with the necessary CAD tools to efficiently
define, detail and produce nearly 1,800 double-
curved wooden glulam segments.

definition for all the different details of a curved facade is even more difficult than solving the problem for just one, nicely orthogonal situation. Third, you have to be precise. If high-tech computer-controlled fabrication equipment is used which is able to work within tolerances of less than a millimetre, the tolerances in the model have to be even smaller. That finally means you have to know about geometry. All the mathematics, so comfortably hidden behind the CAD software's buttons, suddenly has to be dealt with in the form of normal vectors, curvature measures and coordinate transformations.

Parametrics and Complexity

Apart from all that, parametric modelling makes things considerably easier. At first sight, even the notion that parametric models 'reduce' the complexity seems to be true, at least in terms of Kolmogorov's definition of descriptive complexity:[1] a printout of the program code together with a table of all parameter sets needs less paper than all the workshop drawings. But this is misleading: both descriptions define the same degree of complexity, only in different languages. The algorithm is much easier to handle than the

set of drawings – especially when it comes to changes – but it is just a translation of the same description. This translation, however, comes at a cost. It takes energy in the form of brain action to come up with a clever algorithm. And even though the current development of parametric modellers – from Grasshopper to CATIA – removes a bit of the programming hassle, the two main tasks remain the same. First, to abstract from a mass of individual problems to a generic 'class' of solutions with a minimal set of parameters that open a solution space just big enough to accommodate all necessary variants. Second, to instantiate all the individual variants with the correct parameter values. Thus, the work did not simply vanish, it just shifted to a higher level of abstraction: programming instead of drawing. In other words, once the complexity has been introduced into the system by making it curvy and non-regular, it remains present; it can only be handled in better or worse ways.

Mass Customisation

All the parametric planning effort would be largely useless without digitally controlled (CNC) fabrication tools that allow the

production of individual components at almost the price of mass production. Those tools are widely available now, but they are neither small, nor cheap, nor will they respond to the 'file-to-factory' buzzword – at least if you want to build something on a one-to-one scale and not just small gypsum models. If you want to fabricate the curved roofs for Shigeru Ban's Centre Pompidou in Metz (2010) or Nine Bridges Golf Resort in South Korea (2009), the appropriate CNC machine needs its own decent-sized factory building. Owning and running such equipment is a business in and of itself, and requires a substantial investment and specialist knowledge.

Ideally, this knowledge is available in the early design stages in order to optimise the design towards the fabrication method; but usually, it isn't. This is simply because no one knows who is going to be the fabricator and which technology he or she is going to use before the tender is completed. To make matters worse, almost every CNC machine reads a different data format and every fabricator uses a different CAM software, which makes generating the machine data for all the individual parts from the parametric

Shigeru Ban, Nine Bridges Golf Resort, Yeoju, South Korea, 2009
A canopy of woven timber girders shelters the resort clubhouse. Twenty-one slender columns support 32 roof elements, assembled from more than 3,500 intricately detailed glulam segments prefabricated in Switzerland. designtoproduction here created a reference geometry of the roof and generated 3-D models for all 467 different timber components, including the details for almost 15,000 lap joints.

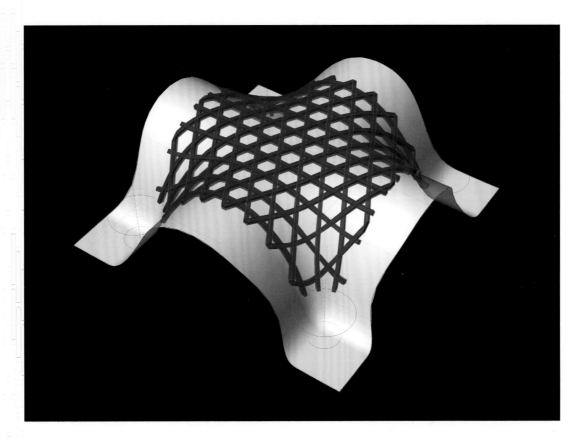

geometry model far from an easy task. The idea of just sending a 3-D model to the fabricator and receiving a few containers full of mass-customised components some days later is downright utopian. At least for all non-standard projects (ordering standard window frames in individual sizes is a different matter), the mass-customisation system that translates the design input into production data has to be developed first. Its details depend on the shape and the intended surface quality, on the materials and fabrication methods used, on the logistics and assembly sequences, on the hardware that is machining the components, and on many more factors. Usually, the whole system is used only once – for the respective project – and then discarded, because at least some of these factors change from project to project, and because designers tend to come up with new challenges in every project.

Obviously, the recent evolution of parametric CAD systems and digital fabrication technologies has made its mark on contemporary architecture. It creates new prospects, but at the same time generates new challenges, mainly due to the immensely increased amount of information that needs to be handled in the planning phase. The integration of knowledge about structure, materials, fabrication and construction into the design is key to the creation of efficient planning and production processes, but let us be honest – this is nothing completely new, it should have always been the lodestar for every good design. Perhaps what has changed is the fact that all this knowledge has to be incorporated into continuously digital production chains that connect design, fabrication and building and ensure the efficient and frictionless flow of all the information, including all necessary translations between different data formats. This is what designtoproduction offers. It will be interesting to see where the ongoing development takes the firm and – in the end – how the profession will be named. ⌂

Note
1. In algorithmic information theory, the Kolmogorov-Complexity of an object is defined by the shortest description of the object in a given language.

Text © 2010 John Wiley & Sons Ltd. Images: pp 86-91, 92(t), 93 © designtoproduction, Zurich/Stuttgart; p 92(b) © Blumer-Lehmann AG Gossau

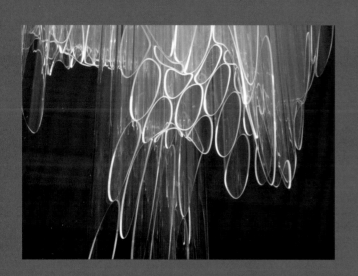

FABRICATING DESIGN
A REVOLUTION OF CHOICE

Frank Barkow

Berlin-based practice Barkow Leibinger has become synonymous with expertise in digital fabrication. For 12 years, the firm has been engaged in designing buildings for machine-tool company Trumpf in Stuttgart – a relationship that has given the firm remarkable insights into the laser cutting of sheet metal. Here, **Frank Barkow** describes the fruitful research that the studio has undertaken in laser cutting as well as two innovative projects that have resulted from it. He explains why a new technology like that of digital fabrication must be for architects by necessity 'a revolution of choice' – a speculation on where best to exploit new possibilities, albeit informed by research and experimentation.

Barkow Leibinger, Light Structure, Hans Peter Jochum Gallery, Berlin, 2009
left: Laser-cut and scripted multicoloured Plexiglas tube lighting array.

opposite: Detail of the lighting array.

Architectural practice is transformed. Emerging production methods and technologies now directly inform architectural construction. It is a revolution of choice. Architects, as never before, are positioned to determine the material and tectonic content of buildings, as desired, independent from standards and convention. Modernist conceits such as modulation, repetition, mass production or serialism give way to the possibility for differentiation, uniqueness and variation as related to economies of production. Technology enables invention. Digital fabrication is an experimental research activity that is embedded in Barkow Leibinger's work and involves a close collaboration between architects, students, engineers and the workshops that support the practice. It is an autonomous activity that facilitates the experimental thinking and making that supports building projects – a speculative and central research discipline that is constantly evolving and being added to.

Design follows technology. Historically, technological change has always driven innovation in design. The challenge for a designer once such capabilities become available is to speculate how to exploit new possibilities that understand the technology, its promise, and its utility beyond expectations. Specifically, a survey of current digital machines leads to a better understanding of new technologies and how they might transform materials. Here tools shape materials that lead to form, and not the other way round. This is a process where active archiving of tools and material processes contribute to an internal catalogue of tectonic possibilities that can then be drawn from for building projects. *Barkow Leibinger: An Atlas of Fabrication* began as a catalogue and exhibition at

the Architectural Association (AA) in London in March 2009[1] that formalised a method to collect research work in a comparative way. This relative autonomy allows such research a speculative bias free from initial constraints of programme or specific utility. Standard building catalogues are replaced by internal expertise in construction systems that are developed and applied to buildings. Situated as a research practice this is the best path to formal invention and authenticity driven by an experimental working environment.

A prototype (defined as an architectural component with both formal and performative characteristics) arises from the specific capacities of a technology when coupled with design opportunity and imagination. A prototype is something new as distinguished from earlier models or attempts. The search for an idea for an architectural prototype emerges from the control of a technical system. Digital fabrication contributes to this by locating computation as a physical process for transforming materials rather than, as in its initial application, the producing of visual images. The strength of the prototype as a working methodology is that it supersedes representational strategies (drawings and scale models) with an artefact that predicts exactly architectural effect. This means a prototype helps to close the historical gap (unpredictability) between representation and built reality by offering a means to simulate it precisely in order to enable change or alteration. Technical rapidity allows quick construction of types to ascertain any values or deficits to be corrected, replacing time-intensive handcrafted mock-ups.

Twelve years of building for the German machine-tool company Trumpf in Stuttgart has given Barkow Leibinger

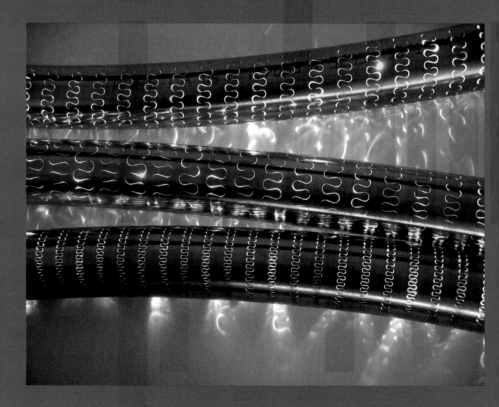

Barkow Leibinger, Coil-Tubes,
Indianapolis Museum of Art, 2008
Detail of coil-tubes showing laser-cut interlocking segments allowing variable flexibility.

an education in how the firm's laser cutting of sheet metal digitally contributes to the making of Trumpf's own buildings. It is a technology that is incredibly latent for architectural application, allowing the revisiting of historical projects begun in the early 20th century by architects such as Jean Prouvé with machines that expand construction possibilities enormously. This is not an exclusive way of working. Wide networks of international fabricators offer endless possibilities. Both analogue and digital processes contribute to diverse approaches to working. It is an evolving process that is expanding and being added to, and is contributing to a field of knowledge and opportunity that has the capacity to shape the very identity of an architectural practice.

It is a technology that is incredibly latent for architectural application, allowing the revisiting of historical projects begun in the early 20th century by architects such as Jean Prouvé with machines that expand construction possibilities enormously.

Laser Cutting

A particularly fruitful research area is the relatively new idea of cutting three-dimensional tube profiles from metal – typically steel, stainless steel or Plexiglass – with revolving laser cutting. Trumpf laser-cutting (Tubematic) machines work standard tubes that are round, square, oval or rectangular in shape that are fed through a cutting environment where a fixed laser-cutting head cuts the material by turning and advancing it, creating complex and unique cut patterns. Additionally, tube profiles can take on complex radial structural shapes when digitally bent or scroll-cut to enable a chain-like sequence of individual segments producing complex catenary curves while the segments remain locked together.

Two characteristics of tube fabrication are apparent. First, by cutting a single profile, multiple complex shapes can be harvested from each tube without any waste of material, as

above: **Cover and page samples from *Barkow Leibinger: An Atlas of Fabrication*, Architectural Association Publications (London), 2009.**

top: Trumpf's Tubematic machine tool in operation cutting stainless-steel tube.

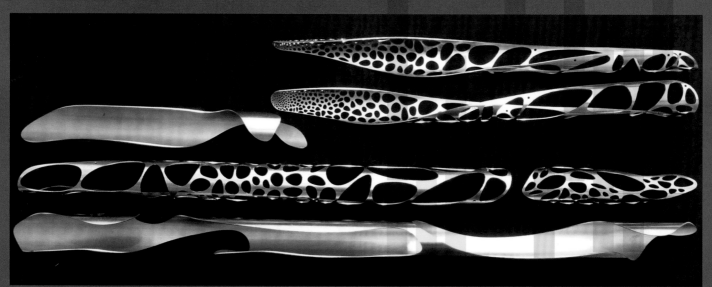

Barkow Leibinger, Tube
Cuts, Exhibition Gallery,
Architectural Association,
London, 2009
above: Laser-cut steel
tube experiments showing
multiple elements from
common source-tube.

Barkow Leibinger,
'Contemplating the Void'
exhibition, Guggenheim
Museum, New York, 2010
top left: Installation proposal of
laser-cut acrylic glass tubes.

Barkow Leibinger, Scenario
facade, Stuttgart, 2009
top right: Laser-cut Corten steel
facade mock-up for the Scenario
commercial fashion building.

is common with cutting two-dimensional flat-sheet stock. Also, unlike two-dimensional cutting of patterns, these shapes are three-dimensionally complex, combining both curved surface and free-form outline (or profile). Second, the tubes are essentially a cellular (volumetrically structural) element that are equally disposed to constructing complex arching frames or can be collected; that is, accumulated to produce bundles. This means that in a series of prototypes or installations, tubes are gathered to create dense bundles of poché, which can then be carved into to create volumetric forms. By dispersing (spacing apart) the tubes' fields, stalk-like arrangements, screens or structural arches can be formed. This technique thus enables ornamental organic shapes to be cut and also extends structural possibilities.

In vertical arrays, tubes rotate mechanically along their long axes, producing complex moiré-like facades that control light and visual transparency or opacity by simply turning arrays simultaneously or individually. By way of bespoke fabrication, an endless amount of variation can be achieved by tooling an off-the-shelf standard construction profile. It is also a building element that is scalable, from small non-structural elements to larger ones with structural capacity. By simply applying multiple scaled building elements, a kind of systematic universality to a construction problem becomes available, rather than an assembly of endless different building components. An accumulating organisational system in this case means that a single repetitive component (a tube profile) can be modified singularly and incrementally, adding up to a larger and more complex volumetric of

formal arrays, a direct outcome of the primary element (unlike a standard brick), that can vary from each other. This is a very different procedure to, for example, using software to produce a form then backloading that form with a material and structural tectonic for realising it.

The Gallery and the Pavilion

The architectural exhibition is a forum that helps situate digital fabrication research. The gallery, as a site for architecture, is no longer relevant for referring to an architecture outside its walls through representations (drawings and models), and is instead primarily for site-specific installations of temporary architecture whose effects are experiential. Such gallery installations depict nothing beyond themselves. They are architectural events in their own right. This halfway house of architectural effect and conjuncture is located between the open-endedness of an initial experiment and an actual building placed in a particular context.

Another vehicle for speculative research is the pavilion type. Temporary and programmatically open-ended and flexible, a pavilion embodies both pragmatic workability and experimental speculation. In 2009, with structural engineer Werner Sobek, Barkow Leibinger designed a tube-steel pavilion for the 25th anniversary of the Deutsches Architekturmuseum (DAM) in the garden of the Museum for Arts and Crafts in Frankfurt am Main. Beginning with sponsored materials (steel tubes and Bayer Makrolon polycarbonate), individual, digitally bent tube types were proposed to produce a complex arched form cross-braced by smaller tubes arching in the opposing direction. Using digital scripting software, the geometry of the form was studied

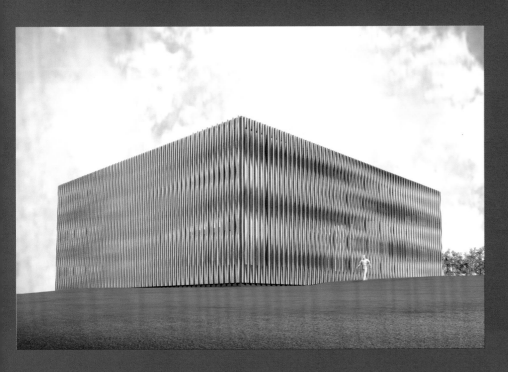

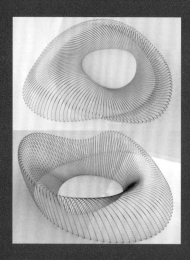

Barkow Leibinger, DAM Pavilion, German Architecture Museum, Frankfurt, 2009
top left: Digital rendering of the structural concept of the pavilion.

top right: The 1:1 steel-tube and polycarbonate shingle mock-up with the model in the foreground.

Barkow Leibinger, Nomadic Garden, 11th Venice Architecture Biennale, 2008
above: Installation detail of movable laser-cut stainless-steel tubes placed on a CNC-cut timber platform.

opposite: Installation for director Aaron Betsky's thematic 'Architecture Beyond Buildings'.

in order to limit a number of overlapping clear Makrolon shingles, allowing both tolerance in the construction and open joints at the shingle to provide ventilation for summer use. Sunshading and power for the pavilion programmes (exhibitions and a café) are provided by sandwiching photovoltaic cells to the shingles. While the recession has delayed construction of the pavilion, an exhibition was organised to construct a 1:1 prototype/segment of it, which proved an essential step in checking the structural and construction viability of the project.

Two recent exhibitions have examined tube arrays as a ground-based field system and as a suspended one. At the 11th Venice Architecture Biennale (2008), Barkow Leibinger presented an installation of clusters of stainless-steel tubes, which created a kind of nomadic garden. The Nomadic Garden installation was organised into a series of gradiating-height pods of scroll-cut tubes that formed a series of paths between them. For the duration of the four-month long exhibition, visitors could rearrange the tubes by pulling them out of a peg-board-like wooden base that was CNC-cut to allow the tubes to fit in an unlimited range of positions. The original arrangement gave way to a haphazard dispersal of local rearrangements of tubes, demonstrating the limits and possibilities of an open-ended system combining digital craft and technique.

For the second exhibition at the Hans Peter Jochum Gallery in Berlin (2009), Barkow Leibinger's Light Structure, a prototypical chandelier, was constructed of multiple clusters of coloured acrylic glass tubes that were laser-cut in order to allow light to transmit through the polished edges the cut produces. Digital scripting allows for two pieces to be produced

by each cut, which then can be tangentially connected to each other creating a continuous web of topographical surfaces formed by the continuous rings abutting each other. These volumetric bundles in both the Venice and Berlin projects create landscapes of complex geometry supported by a reconfigured base module, which is an off-the-shelf tube.

Material research is an evolving process that assumes a central position in Barkow Leibinger's practice. This is a conviction that architectural ideas and materials are mutually integrated with one other: 'Architecture is a physical substance, and the point of conceptualization is to figure out how to treat that material. Such an approach is predicated on the inevitability of architecture as a construction, and argues that conception begins with an understanding of the building's physical dimension.'[2]

Experimentation is the point at which imagination mediates with knowledge. This is what gives Barkow Leibinger's work its identity. It empowers architects to locate themselves precisely at the point where they have the best chance of predicting and controlling the effect of their buildings. It is an incredibly fascinating and challenging point in time at which the trajectories of emerging technologies, materiality, sustainability and imagination all intersect. ᴆ

Notes
1. See *Barkow Leibinger: An Atlas of Fabrication*, Architectural Association Publications (London), 2009.
2. George Wagner, *Matters of Fact: The Architecture of Barkow Leibinger*, Werkbericht , Birkhäuser (Basel), 2001, p 11.

Text © 2010 John Wiley & Sons Ltd. Images: p 94(l) © Sue Barr/AA; pp 94-5 © Corinne Rose; pp 96, 97(b), 98-9, 100(t) © Barkow Leibinger Architects; p 97(t) © TRUMPF GmbH + Co KG; p 100(b), 101 © Amy Barkow/Barkow Photo

TIMBERFABRIC

APPLYING TEXTILE PRINCIPLES
ON A BUILDING SCALE

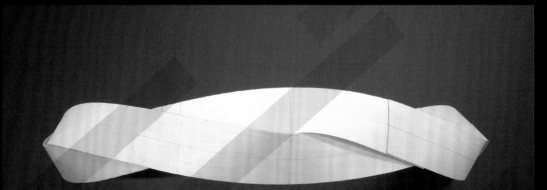

**Markus Hudert, Textile
Module, EPFL IBOIS, 2008**
opposite top: Model of the Textile
Module. The Textile Module acts
as unit cell for different kinds of
Timberfabric structures.

*opposite bottom, below
and bottom*: Braided arch.
Top, perspective and front
view of braided arch based
on the Textile Module.

Timber is coming to the fore as a contemporary construction material.
Not only sustainable, its suppleness, adaptability and strength make it
highly attractive for experimental designers. Yves Weinand founded the
interdisciplinary timberfabric research project at IBOIS, the Laboratory for
Timber Fabric, at the École Polytechnique Fédérale de Lausanne (EPFL), in
order to fully explore innovative timber construction techniques. Here **Yves
Weinand and Markus Hudert** describe the Textile Module, which Hudert
developed, in order to investigate timber's ability for 'social behaviour', or
greater structural strength, once woven into a textile-like form.

Practical and material orientated academic research has become increasingly important for architectural practice, due to several factors. First, it contributes to contemporary concepts in architecture and improves their implementation. Today's architects are looking for a deeper understanding of technical and technological questions related to architecture: technology, construction methods and structural considerations are no longer seen as merely bothersome necessities, as was often the case in the past. The importance of such aspects and the potential of including them as active stimuli in the architectural design process are largely recognised. It is the limitations in time and capacities that more often than not confound the realisation of such ambitions. Academic research can fill this gap and provide architectural practices with the necessary resources.

Second, research has a duty to address one of the biggest architectural challenges of our time; namely, how to achieve sustainable building. Society's burgeoning awareness of the urgent need to use renewable materials for building construction is an undeniable reality and has become an important parameter for architectural production. As a result, timber constructions experience a new popularity and the importance of research on timber has increased. The potential of this field becomes evident with some of its latest developments and innovations. Cross-laminated timber panels open up new dimensions for massive timber construction and prefabrication in context with the digital chain. Technologies such as wood welding and the densification of wood create new possibilities not only for architecture but also for furniture and product design. Timber as a building material is therefore capable of satisfying both the demands of contemporary architecture and the requirements of sustainable building.

The Timberfabric research project pursues an interdisciplinary approach and links the three domains of architecture, structural engineering and timber construction. The research opens the way to a new era of innovative timber constructions and timber construction techniques. It initiates an unprecedented exploration and study of timber-related structures, their structural analysis and how the principles of textiles can be applied to their design.

The inherent characteristics of wood present an important precondition for this undertaking. It can be classified as both a soft and viscous material, with suppleness as one of its properties. Both wood and fabrics can be seen as fibre-based tissues, which makes for an interesting investigation of the analogy between micro-scale fibre structures and timber-derived wooden structures on multiple levels.

Wood is basically composed of a multitude of cellulose fibres. The fibres are flexible, allowing for respectively elastic deformation. Until now, the capacity for producing curved glued-laminated timber beams has not led to a broader application of this property for timber, but in fact the implications are profound. Indeed, timber has the dual capacities to be formed and to retain a given form. The application of textile principles in the context of timber construction creates a fascinating association of intrinsically contrasting physical conditions. Traditionally, building structures have striven for rigidity whereas textiles embody the properties of elasticity and suppleness. It is of more than anecdotal interest that, for one of the first Timberfabric prototypes, it was impossible to

determine an ultimate load-bearing capacity. While exposed to an increasing load, its elasticity enabled it to perform dramatic deformation and to evade its destruction. The ability of a structure to adapt to a load is a highly interesting property that will be subject to further investigations in the future.

Textiles have yet another quality that is of relevance for building structures. They are composed of a multitude of yarn elements that work cooperatively together as one entity. In this kind of 'social behaviour', in the case of failure of the weakest element this will not provoke the collapse of the structure as a whole since the load of the weakest element will be carried by those adjacent to it. The implication is that structures using the same principle will have a higher security factor than that of traditional ones.

An entity composed of a multitude of elements offers further possibilities. Differentiated repetition of the basic elements can create an immense number of variations of the total structure and each one of them can be optimised. Thus it can be expected that the generation of novel structures with highly specific performance profiles, characterised by lightness and robustness in an equal manner, will be feasible.

The Textile Module

It is obvious that the basic unit of the repeating structure is essential for the development of structural timber fabrics. Here, the Timberfabric research currently focuses on the application of the Textile Module, the geometry of which is generated by interbraiding two planar timber panels. The use of a particular technique of assembly, together with the specific material properties, leads towards a structurally efficient construct. Here, a major difference to common contemporary processes of architectural production and form generation becomes evident. Commonly, digital processes are used to inform seamless virtual matter, whose properties have no relation to those of real materials. Physical matter is treated as a passive compound, a mere means to an end, and form is obtruded upon it. The influence of scale upon material properties is ignored.

In contrast to this, the strategy applied here of treating material, formal and structural aspects on the same level is likely to produce exceptional structural solutions. While the focus of these studies applies specifically to timber, they should also give incentives to the use of other materials and applications. The material's physical properties are considered as an active parameter of the design process. This consideration also underlines the importance of physical modelling within this research. Standard software is currently not able to simulate material behaviour such as elastic deformation, but the development of software that can do so is an essential step in connecting the Textile Module with digital planning and production. Inputs from mathematics and mechanical engineering are necessary to successfully execute this part of the work.

Structural Analysis

Mathematical and mechanical engineering inputs are also required for the structural analysis of building-scale timber fabric. A stage of preliminary investigations is thus necessary. In order to establish proper analytical models of such structures, a clear understanding of their geometry is required.

Markus Hudert, Timberfabric prototype based on the Textile Module, EPFL IBOIS, 2009

left: The Textile Module can be combined in many different ways. In this version, two layers of braided arches are superimposed, augmenting the structural height and enabling indirect lighting.

Markus Hudert, Different configurations of Timberfabric EPFL IBOIS, 2008

below: Different configurations of Timberfabric. Structural timber fabrics are composed of a multitude of small, interconnected structural elements. Such structures, based on iterative elements, exhibit 'social behaviour'. The failure of one or several basic elements does not provoke the collapse of the structure as a whole, since elements adjacent to the failed ones take over their load. As a consequence it can be expected that structural timber fabrics have a higher security factor than traditional structures.

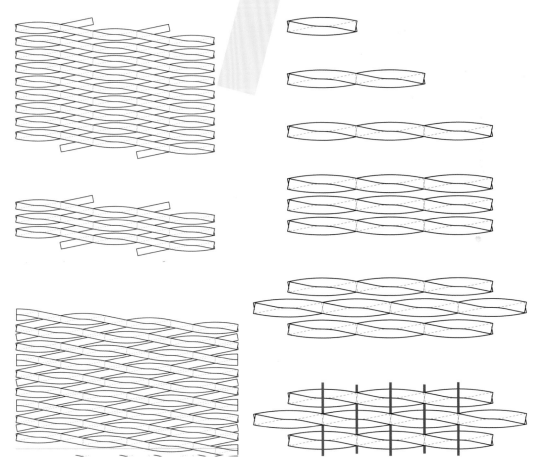

Architectural production over the
past decade has been marked by
a strong affection for the image.
The seductive aesthetics of digital
architectural modelling and
visualisation have often dominated
over attention towards materiality
and building construction.

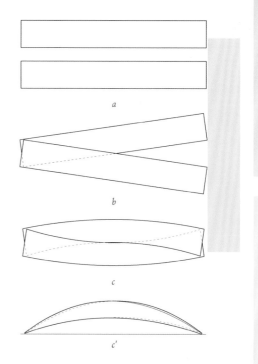

a

b

c

c'

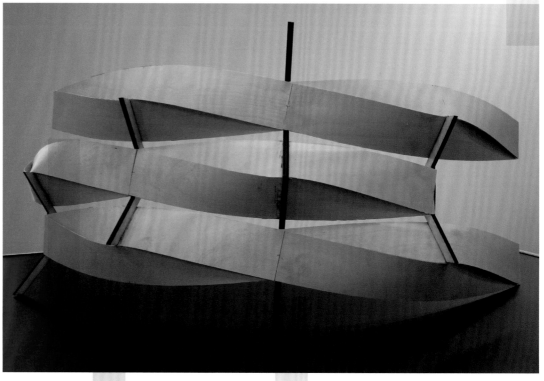

**Markus Hudert, Timberfabric
prototype with interacting warps
and wefts, EPFL IBOIS, 2008**
above and opposite: Warps and
wefts. Several braided arches
interact with elements in the
perpendicular direction. In textile
terms, this woven structure
incorporates warps and wefts.

top: Assembly process of the
Textile Module. The geometry is
generated by using the process
of braiding as an assembly
technique. The correlation of
technique, material and form
make it a coherent object.

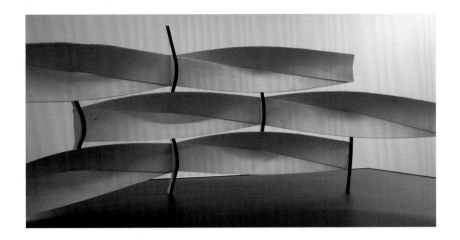

In general, the intention is to use initially plane timber panels as the starting material. During the process of assembly these become double curved, the imposed deformations lead to initial stresses, caused by bending and torsion moments, and specific questions arise for which quantitative answers can be determined. Which radius is required? Which curvature can be accepted? An empirical approach, using a series of physical models, is applied to address such questions. The further structural investigations necessary are based on these preliminary observations.

In this context, the question of scale is essential. Various questions related to the material used arise while proceeding with such scale jumps from small models to building scale. It is therefore important to obtain more knowledge about such scale factors and how they affect the spatial and mechanical behaviour of structures. It has been observed that at large scale, the prototypes are subject to a higher flexibility and dynamic sensibility. It is possible to define a specific, dynamic calculation for a specific structure at a given scale. But it has not yet been possible to define parameters that describe the optimisation of these structures through different scales while keeping every proportion the same. Furthermore, the underlying rules, determining how such transitions occur or when they occur, are not yet identified. The study of this fascinating topic involves a very precise recording of the changing behaviour and interaction of the basic elements of structural timber fabric across the different scales. A profound examination of this phenomenon is crucial.

The first set of observations that need to be made are systematic comparisons between the initial structure and the deformed structure for every given structural proposal or geometry. Geometrical and mechanical observations need to be collected. The deformation process creates a specific stress situation, which can be described as 'initial stress'. Those parameters can be measured by means of computer simulation, where the deformation process is modelled. The initial stress situation can be established via measures taken directly on the physical prototype by stress-sensing elements. Once the initial stress situation is known, various load cases can be performed giving more insight into the structural performance of a given Timberfabric. The interaction of the curved elements occurs in such a way that it confers a specific rigidity to this type of structure even though the basic element seems to be quite smooth. In pilot studies of prototypes, particular structural

behaviours have been observed, such as an increase of the rigidity of a given woven section while applying a load to it. Here, the section's inertia increased during the loading process because of the structure's capacity to be deformed. Such observations open very exciting perspectives for the utility of structural optimisation processes.

The Imagined and the Material
Architectural production over the past decade has been marked by a strong affection for the image. The seductive aesthetics of digital architectural modelling and visualisation have often dominated over attention towards materiality and building construction. Ambivalent images were, and still are, produced with digital tools. They display architectural visions that neglect the constraints of the physical laws and the constraints associated with building construction.[1] Yet we know that architecture is not, and cannot be, just an image. It has become evident that such proposals are extremely difficult to realise. It has also become evident that the potential of the computer as a planning and design tool has its limitations. In the same time, innovative applications of non-digital means of design have come to provide interesting alternatives.[2] The approach applied in the IBOIS research goes beyond the aesthetics of an imagined reality. Materiality is actively involved in the design process. The Textile Module is an intriguing first result and encourages continuing the adopted direction. Its aesthetic and structural qualities have raised a wide range of questions, many of which are still to be addressed. There appears to be something remarkable in the interaction of the material and the formal qualities that produces a distinguished quality of design. It is not clear whether the topological or tectonic properties are a satisfying answer to this. It is perhaps the elevation of materiality to a level of prominence in design and design research that can explain this intellectual resonance and its implications for architecture as a material practice. ∆

Notes
1. This was, for instance, the case with an image related to Dagmar Richter's DR_D lab project, The Living Museum: Pimp my Architecture (2005), published on the cover of *AD Architextiles* (Vol 76, No 6, 2006). Here, a highly appealing image is presented, but one cannot understand how what is shown could possibly be built, or materialised.
2. A very interesting approach to this was proposed by Mark West in his article 'Thinking With Matter', published in *AD Protoarchitecture* (Vol 78, No 4, 2008).

Text © 2010 John Wiley & Sons Ltd. Images © Markus Hudert, EPFL IBOIS

Fabio Gramazio
Matthias Kohler
Silvan Oesterle

ENCODING MATERIAL

Gramazio & Kohler's work in the faculty of Architecture and Digital Fabrication at ETH Zurich is renowned for its pioneering work with industrial robots. Here, **Fabio Gramazio, Matthias Kohler and Silvan Oesterle** describe how the integration of fabrication-relevant decisions into encoded designs enables the control of complex interactions between material elements and facilitates the direct generation of machine data, as epitomised by their West Fest Pavilion project.

Gramazio & Kohler (Architecture and Digital Fabrication, ETH Zurich), West Fest Pavilion, Zurich, 2009
The wood battens have been connected by screws, reducing the pre-tensioning, which results in thinner battens and less material consumption.

Gramazio & Kohler (Architecture and Digital Fabrication, ETH Zurich), The Sequential Wall, Zurich, 2008
below: The Sequential Wall elective course investigates the architectonic and constructive potential of additive digital fabrication in timber construction. The interplay of many small parts results in a material system whose properties in terms of function and design go beyond the individual batten module.

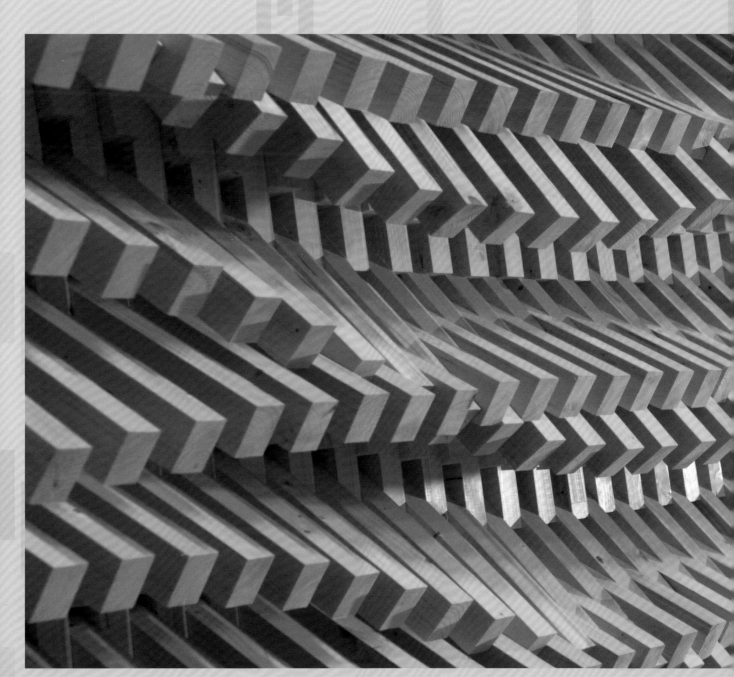

opposite top: The end-effector
of the robot corresponds with
custom export and design
scripts that link the physical
machine with digital data.

The use of computer-controlled
production tools already available but
typically underused in construction
trades provides new opportunities for
a freedom of design that is innovative
and adheres to constructional logic
at the same time.

We are in the midst of a period of major change in the
production conditions in architecture. Over the last 20 years
it has become possible to industrially manufacture individual,
non-standardised elements according to their digital
delineation. As a result, architects have started to integrate
fabrication as a generative paradigm into the design process.
During the period of early Modernism in architecture there
were similar tendencies, for example the Bauhaus School's
principle 'art and technology – a new entity'. This resulted
in an architecture that exploited the possibilities of industrial
production to achieve satisfactory design standards, regarding
both functional and aesthetic aspects. It found an expression
for the possibilities of the machine age and its control over
fabrication information which was repetitive and standardised.

The use of computer-controlled production tools already
available but typically underused in construction trades
provides new opportunities for a freedom of design that is
innovative and adheres to constructional logic at the same
time. The material element and the fabrication machine
inform the building process and provide the parameters
and constraints for the design process. The integration of
fabrication-relevant decisions into encoded designs allows the
architect to control complex interactions between singular
material elements and facilitates the direct generation of
machining data. This implies the understanding of physical
conditions of architecture as well as material properties
as the foundation for design programming that develops
from drawing geometric elements into defining material
components and their assembly logic. Thus a design-focused
relationship between the digital and the material can emerge.[1]

The End-Effector

With direct access to the definition of material systems
through programming manufacturing data, the question
arises: Which are the relevant tools that allow the fabrication
of building-scale elements and are flexible enough to adapt to
different materials and assembly logics? The digital description
of an object to be built can be extremely specific and can
consist of a multitude of different instructions. Designing with
assembly logic develops its full potential in combination with

Gramazio & Kohler (Architecture and
Digital Fabrication, ETH Zurich), West
Fest Pavilion, Zurich, 2009
The interior lighting supports the
appearance of the overlaps in the middle
of the column that gradually attenuate
according to the vertical forces.

a manufacturing machine capable of physically carrying out different actions. An industrial robot meets this requirement on an architectural building scale. It is a generic tool and not specialised for one specific activity. The robot has a universal arm that can reach any point in three-dimensional space. The actual tool, an end-effector that defines the material machining process, is attached to the end of this kinematic chain. The manufacturing process thus consists of the data required to control the robot and the respective properties of the tool being used. The design and development of custom end-effectors is important as it enables the architect to reach into the conception of material processes.

Expanding Design Information Content

The connection of digital fabrication and computation enables the immediate programming of production data and directly links the design with the making of architecture. As a result the architect can fully control the construction process down to the smallest detail. This enables increasing the building components' information level, which consists, first, of a large set of individual parts that make up the components and their joints. Second, it may include information about functional and material aspects. The question arises of how to deal with this on the one hand powerful, but on the other hand critical, direct relation of design and construction. If the programming of detail systems is within the control of the architect, new potential for the design is possible. The architect's design data does not need to be converted to construction instructions by a number of different parties involved in the building process, but can be used for fabrication as is.

A mere rationalisation of workflow might discard the creative potential that could emerge from the interdependence of design and fabrication. Only through the configuration of detail systems that encapsulate the increasing amount of material and fabrication parameters within simple and manageable methods can a new design space evolve. This allows designing with the specific characteristics of a building process and at the same time shaping the process itself. In this case, one should be aware that a major difference exists between

the precise numeric design and the physical world – geometric and fabrication data do not contain information about physical conditions such as gravity or material properties per se. Conversely, this means anticipating physical requirements at the outset of the parametric design process and using material conditions as well as assembly logics as the basis for coding.

Design Information and the Structure of Construction

The West Fest Pavilion project (2009)[2] explores which criteria of a material system are decisive for architecture and how the correlation of differing requirements can offer new design potential. Standard wooden battens are stacked up to form columns that transform into a roof. The robotic fabrication allows the modification of the length of individual battens during the production process before placing them in their final position in space. The columns constitute the spatial layout as well as the carrying structure of the pavilion, which are both determined by the architectural organisation of the programme, the structural performance and the assembly process.

The driving forces of the structural system are a minimal joining surface between the layers that transfers vertical compression loads, and an appropriate connection method that allows tractive forces coming from wind loads to be received. Through coding the assembly logic, the interrelation of the aforementioned constraints becomes possible and leads to new architectural solutions. For example, the overlap in the middle of a column's side maintains the minimum overlap required to transfer vertical loads and adheres to the maximum batten length. As a result the column's weight is reduced through dissolving the structure towards the top. This has several advantages. Firstly it reduces the self-weight on the lower parts of the column, and secondly it permits a larger cantilever to form the roof. Thirdly, and most important, it allows accentuating the wooden materiality through indirect lighting inside the column. The batten's overlap that shapes the ornamentation of the night lighting is a direct effect of the structural system and the way the vertical forces are transferred through the structure.

left: The columns were fabricated off site. Each column is individually rotated, producing a progression of subtly varied spaces. The detailing of the edges accentuates the rotation through the jagged overlap that at the same time prevents the wood from splintering under tractive forces.

below: The pavilion columns were fabricated from simple wooden battens by a robot that cut and stacked them. Three elements formed one column. Shown here is the topmost one where the element starts to dissolve towards the corners.

bottom: The pavilion was conceived as a temporary spatial structure for a major public event hosted by the canton of Zurich. The wooden structure consists of 16 contorted elements made from 372 wooden battens.

Gramazio & Kohler (Architecture
and Digital Fabrication, ETH
Zurich), The Sequential Wall,
Zurich, 2008
bottom: Standard wooden battens
are cut to length and stacked to
form a building shell. Functional
requirements of an external
timber wall such as insulation and
constructive weather protection had
to be addressed. The gap between
the inner and outer layer can be
filled with insulation material.
Individual protruding battens form
a sacrificial layer and drain water
off the external facade.

below right: The wall combines a
shielding exterior surface with a
girder-like structure. The rippling at the
tip of the battens allows them to be
connected to the load-bearing parts.

below left: Two generative
design systems – a perforated
and a closed one – correlate
to form a coherent whole. The
singular components allow
for a flexible transition at the
borderline of the two systems.

below right: Individual
wooden battens that protruded
outwards and face down
were used to shield the
structural parts from water by
channelling it away from the
facade in much the same way
as pine needles or shingles do.

Expanding and Programming the Performance of Material Systems

Even when the number of functional requirements of a building element increases it is possible to address them with simple material components. Algorithmic design systems enable the selective manipulation of fabrication data whereby material can be structured according to its properties and functional requirements. The singular material elements are augmented with information that can enhance their performance. This results in more complex design and fabrication data. In order to operate in this ever increasing set of information, logical systems must be designed that define and codify the material and structural relationships of the individual elements to each other. In the elective semester course The Sequential Wall taught at ETH Zurich (2008),[3] wood battens are stacked up to form walls. The fabrication process is similar to the West Fest Pavilion project, but the walls need to provide for the performance requirements of an exterior building shell: constructive weather protection and thermal insulation.

In order to increase the material potential of a system made from simple wood battens, physical experiments are exploited to define their arrangement and scope of variation. For example, watering tests define the possible range of overlaps and lengths within the water-bearing layer. This information is abstracted into design algorithms, which results in the interplay of many small parts that form a constructive system whose properties in terms of function and design go beyond the individual batten module. Although the controlled interplay of complex material arrangements cannot surpass the functionality of a highly specialised constructive layer, it can yield an effective combination of simple material parts to form high-performance building elements.

CNC: Crafting Numerical Control

Achieving a sophisticated building component with a simple material and connection through a high level of knowledge of construction techniques can be compared to methods used by manufacturers from pre-industrialised ages. Despite the similarities, today the action of material handling is indirect through the use of numerically controlled machines as opposed to the instant feedback about the work in progress the skilled manufacturer received through the tool in his hand. With computer-aided manufacturing (CAM), the tool is controlled through explicit routing data, which leaves no room for interpretation and adaptation. This change of workflow redefines the interface between architect and manufacturer. The manufacturer becomes a specialist in operating CNC machines and the architect designs control data for these machines. To derive solutions that effectively negotiate between beauty and construction without resorting to unmanageable complexity, the architect and the manufacturer must collaborate. The architect needs to be knowledgeable about the production conditions and able to integrate the implicit knowledge of the trades he or she is working with into the design of explicit machining code.

These changes in production conditions and working processes lead to the assumption that new forms of architectonic expressions will emerge. They require appreciation for the elegance of construction that is less based on demonstrating the perfected functionality of each singular building element, but should negotiate differing functional requirements of architectural components to form a coherent synthesis of material and design system. ⌂

Notes
1. For further reading, see Fabio Gramazio and Matthias Kohler, *Digital Materiality In Architecture: Gramazio and Kohler*, Lars Müller Publishers (Baden), 2008.
2. Gramazio & Kohler, Architecture and Digital Fabrication, ETH Zurich, 2009. Collaborators: Roman Kallweit, Michael Knauß, Ralph Bärtschi, Michael Lyrenmann.
3. Gramazio & Kohler, Architecture and Digital Fabrication, ETH Zurich, 2008. Collaborators: Silvan Oesterle, Ralph Bärtschi, Michael Lyrenmann. Students: Michael Bühler, David Dalsass, Simon Filler, Milena Isler, Roman Kallweit, Morten Krog, Ellen Leuenberger, Jonas Nauwelaertz de Agé, Jonathan Roider, Steffen Samberger, Chantal Thomet, Rafael Venetz and Nik Werenfels.

Text © 2010 John Wiley & Sons Ltd. Images: pp 108-9, 112, 113(b) © Roman Keller; pp 110-11, 113(tr), 114-15 © Gramazio & Kohler, ETH Zurich; p 113(tl) © Mark Röthlisberger

*Martin
Bechthold*

THE RETURN OF THE FUTURE

A SECOND GO AT ROBOTIC CONSTRUCTION

The last few years have witnessed a robotic revival with a reinvigoration of interest in what the robot can offer the construction industry. **Martin Bechthold** looks back at the first robotic boom during the 1980s and 1990s when millions of Japanese yen were invested in developing robots that could address the shortage of construction labour. Bechthold further explores the similarities and dissimilarities of the current and previous periods of activity, as supported by his research at Harvard's Graduate School of Design (GSD).

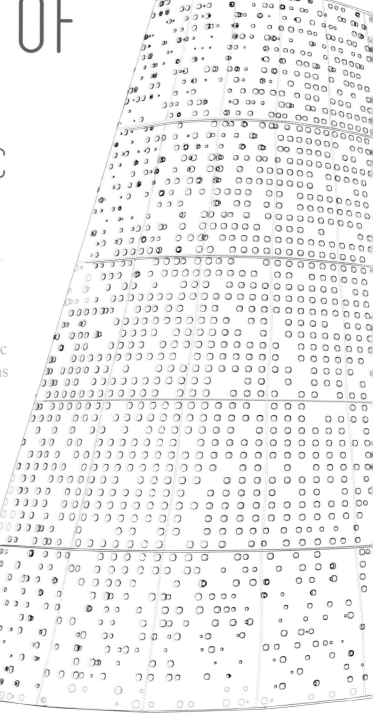

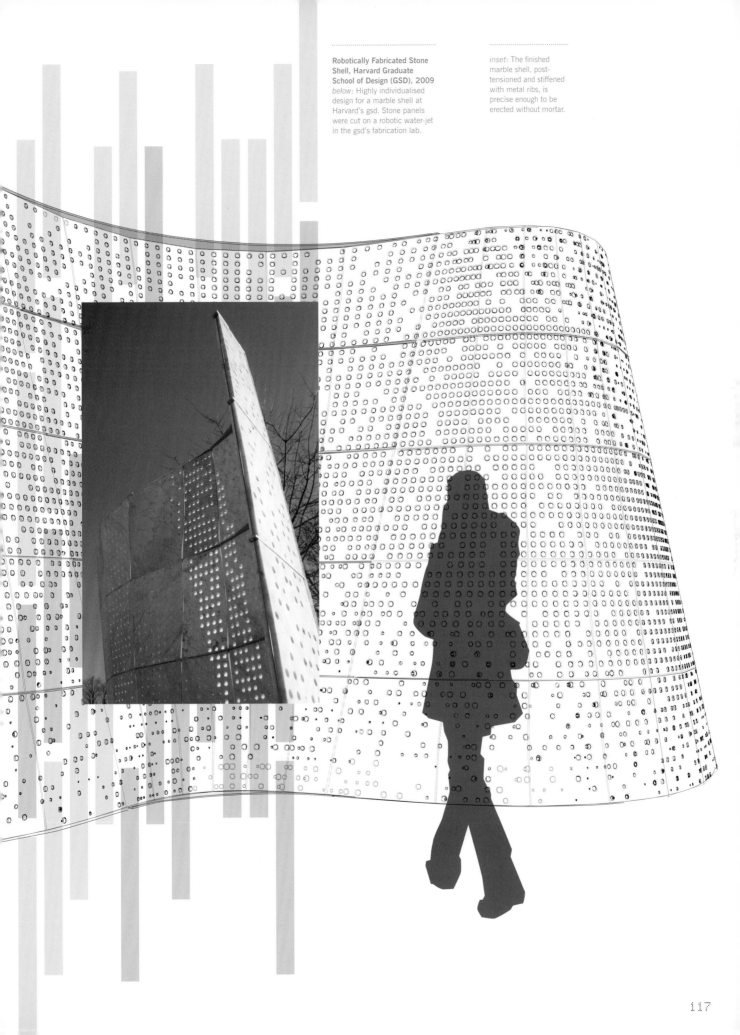

**Robotically Fabricated Stone
Shell, Harvard Graduate
School of Design (GSD), 2009**
below: Highly individualised
design for a marble shell at
Harvard's gsd. Stone panels
were cut on a robotic water-jet
in the gsd's fabrication lab.

inset: The finished
marble shell, post-
tensioned and stiffened
with metal ribs, is
precise enough to be
erected without mortar.

Obayashi Corporation,
Automated Building Construction
System (ABCS), Undisclosed
location, Asia, 2006
below: The ABCS employs
automated cranes and material
delivery systems located at the
top of the high-rise building
under construction.

Toyota Home Factory,
Nagoya area, Japan, 2010
right: Production of
manufactured housing in one
of Toyota Home's factories
in Japan. Lean production
techniques are applied to
a modular design based
on simple structural steel
frames. Robotic devices such
as the welding robot shown
here are extensively used.

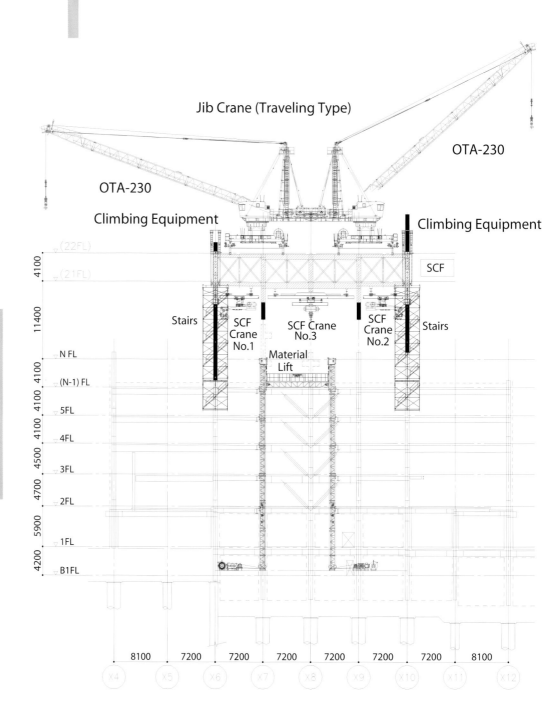

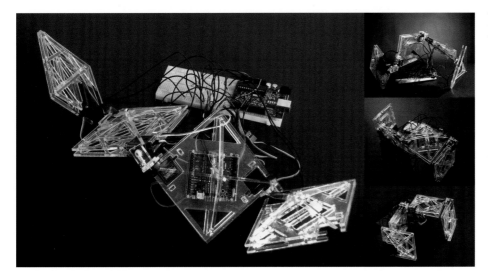

Taro Narahara, Local Control Strategy
for Mobile Robot, Harvard Graduate
School of Design (GSD), 2008
left and below: Taro Narahara, a
doctoral candidate at Harvard's
GSD, developed a robotic device
with locally embedded sensors and
microcontrollers. Bottom-up control
strategies allow the device to optimise
its orientation with respect to a light
source, independent of how and
where the unit is placed. Similar
bottom-up strategies can be applied
to a wide range of digital and
physical applications.

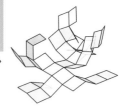

Robotic construction is back, and it may be here to stay. Compared with earlier construction robots, current robotic fabrication involves less problem solving and more design exploration. But what exactly happened to the robotic construction systems of the 1980s and 1990s, the vast majority of which originated in Japan where an estimated 200 were developed?

In the 1980s the Japanese economy was running at full throttle, and construction could barely keep up with demand. But for a generation of young Japanese, working on construction sites was not particularly attractive. Construction work was associated with the '3 Ks': *kiken* (dangerous), *kitanai* (dirty) and *kitsui* (hard). The lack of interest in construction jobs was aggravated by the quickly ageing population that further reduced the pool of young people suitable for the work. A shrinking workforce was therefore the most immediate threat for the future of Japanese construction.

In response the industry dedicated significant resources to developing systems for replacing human labour on site, while at the same time improving productivity and construction quality. A wide range of specialised robotic machines were built and tested for applications such as spray-on fireproofing, concrete placing or finishing, welding or painting. Most remarkable in scale and ambition were the highly automated construction systems that literally 'extruded' high-rise buildings. Over years of development, millions of dollars were spent on creating essentially on-site factory environments with a high degree of automation and robotic support. Weather-sealed workspaces were served by automated gantry cranes and lifting equipment. Automated, laser-based surveying systems provided quality control in real time. Member connections were redesigned to facilitate robotic assembly and robotic welding. The construction process was managed based on 3-D digital models and complex workflow management systems.[1]

Archigram's vision of self-assembling buildings had finally made it into reality. But it became increasingly difficult to justify the development of costly and highly customised automation systems and robots. This first generation of construction robots attempted to replace human labour with robotic action. What proved successful in other industries (such as automotive production) turned out to be extremely difficult for messy and constantly changing construction sites. Replacing humans required sophisticated vision and sensing abilities that were computationally extremely demanding and barely commercially feasible. The early construction robots were custom-built, highly expensive devices, and the value created by their work (spray-on fireproofing, welding) was minimal compared to the investment needed. As a consequence, the technical excellence was never matched by economic success.[2] The projected lack of construction workers lost urgency when the Japanese economic bubble burst in the late 1990s. Research and development budgets shrank quickly and there was little opportunity for exporting the technology – the world was not ready for construction robots.

But is it ready now? Today the emphasis on customisation has been reversed. In the 1980s the tools were custom and the tasks standardised with little value added. Now standard industrial robots perform highly customised tasks that add significant value. Powerful industrial robots are available at a fraction of the cost of a custom robot of the 1980s. The capabilities of today's industrial robots are impressive, and automated fabrication environments can be set up in weeks rather than years. This is true for complex factory automation as well as for custom fabrication approaches.

Parametrically Folded Metal Ceiling, Harvard Graduate School of Design (GSD), 2009
below and bottom left: The parametrically varied design for an undulating ceiling generated a pattern of flat metal shapes that were robotically cut.

opposite: A metal-bending work cell was set up to produce all individual metal forms. A code generator was programmed to create robot instructions directly from the parametric model.

bottom right: The final installation tests highly individualised metal fabrication.

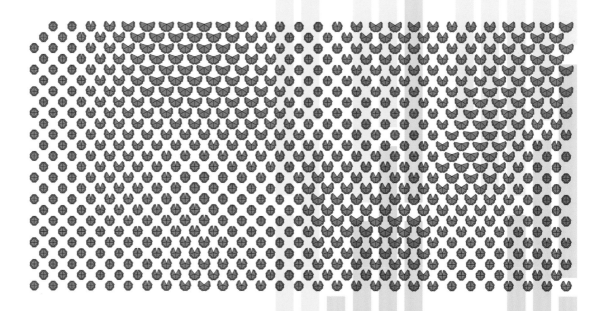

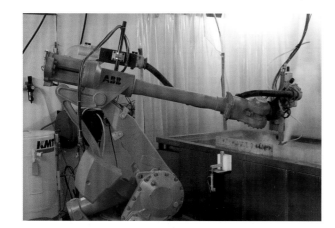

Initial academic research has tended towards producing non-standard assemblies using normative construction materials, and fabricators are also beginning to deploy industrial robots. Major challenges exist on the software rather than the hardware side. Controlling the many arms and movable elements of a robotic manipulator involves challenging issues of collision avoidance, singularities, payload restrictions and repeatability tolerances. In the highly automated car industry, the time spent programming robots is recovered by spreading the cost over high production volumes. The programming of robots for customised construction, on the other hand, deals with much smaller production volumes and the development of newly efficient, automated programming strategies becomes crucial.

Research at Harvard's Graduate School of Design (GSD) studies parametric design and related robotic fabrication methods for schemes that involve many similar, but not equal, parts. The complexity of non-standard parts is addressed by automating the generation of robotic code directly from parametric design models, thus eliminating intermediate software environments. Harvard's Robotically Fabricated Stone Shell (2009), a post-tensioned marble shell with 94 individually shaped and perforated marble panels, served as an early prototype for this approach.[3] The Parametrically Folded Metal Ceiling (2009) prototypes for a highly variable sheet-metal surface, currently under development, have successfully demonstrated the ability to automate the programming of a prototypical robotic sheet-metal environment, with the highly individualised sheet-metal components cut on a robotic water-jet.[4]

Despite the differences between robotic fabrication today and the construction robotics of the 1980s and 1990s, there are similarities. For example, both approaches rely on a unidirectional information flow from design model to code generator and ultimately to the robotic manipulator. A radically different approach to addressing the complexity of design and robotic fabrication systems are bottom-up strategies that rely on local processing and control. Early studies show promising robustness and adaptability, albeit yet unproved in the fabrication context.

Robotic fabrication is the future, to complement conventional construction methods and craft-based fabrication. Chisels and robots do not exclude each other; they each have their place. As robots re-enter construction it is crucial to know when and when not to use them. ⚙

Notes
1. The sheer dimensions of these on-site factories were impressive: their weights ranged between 1,000 and 2,000 tons, and assembly and disassembly took one to two months. The most recent deployment of construction automation systems was Obayashi Corporation's construction of a 22-storey high-rise building completed in 2006.
2. In some cases the efficiency of the robot itself became an obstacle to its commercialisation. Machines such as Shimizu Corporation's robot for spray-on fireproofing (1984–6) proved so efficient that 60 machines sufficed to satisfy the entire Japanese requirement. Without exports the technology was economically doomed.
3. The project was a collaboration between the author and Monica Ponce de Leon and Wes McGee. The Harvard GSD students involved were Jessica Lissagor, Trevor Patt, Damon Sidel, Heather Boesch and Mathieu Blanchard.
4. The project began as part of a course taught by the author. The GSD students involved are Justin Lavallee, Rachel Vroman, Brett Albert, Yair Keshet, Sola Grantham, Jessica Rosenkrantz, Mark Storch and Anthony DiMari,

Text © 2010 John Wiley & Sons Ltd. Images: pp 116-17 © President and Fellows of Harvard College; inset © Martin Bechthold; p 118(t) © Toyota Housing Corporation; p 118(b) © Yuichi Ikeda; p 119 © Taro Narahara; pp 120-1 © Justin Lavallee and Rachel Vroman

A DEEPER
STRUCTURAL
THEORY

The architectural critic and author **Nina Rappaport** celebrates
a new structural synthesis that takes a holistic approach to
tectonics, uniting the bones or structure of a building with its
skin. She calls for a new structurally based theory that effectively
fuses culture and technology, embracing 'deep decoration' and
'subtle innovation' and reviving a design tradition that can be
traced back to AWN Pugin and John Ruskin.

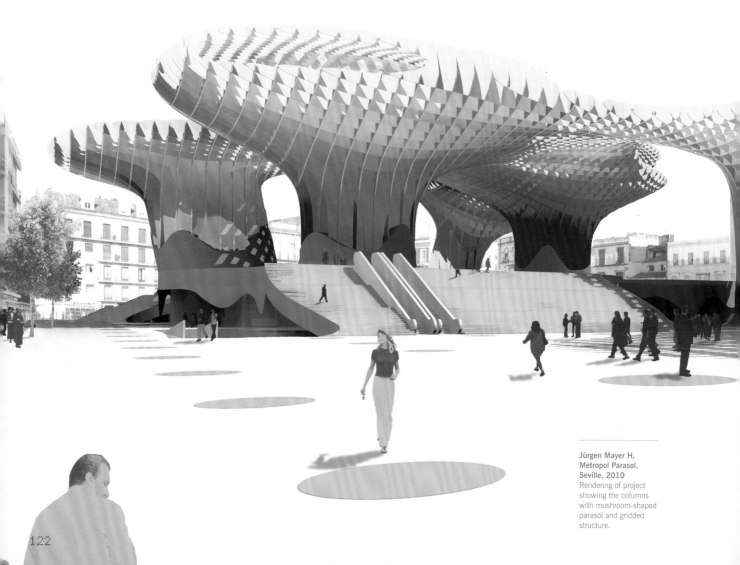

Jürgen Mayer H,
Metropol Parasol,
Seville, 2010
Rendering of project
showing the columns
with mushroom-shaped
parasol and gridded
structure.

Matthew Ritchie, Aranda/
Lasch and Daniel Bosia
(Arup AGU), *The Dawn
Line*, Phase 2, Arup
Gallery, London, 2009
below: Cellular modules
complete the sculptural
ensemble.

Reiser + Umemoto with
Ysrael A Seinuk, O-14
Tower, Dubai, 2010
right: Integrated systems
and structure in the
high-rise.

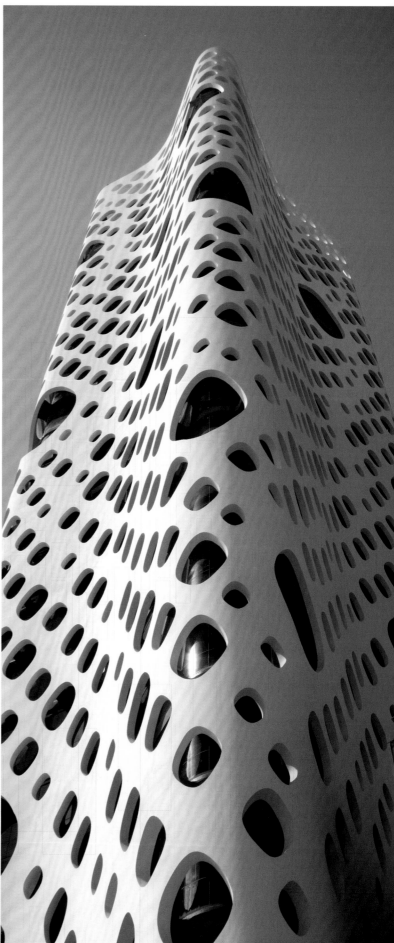

Naum Gabo, Sculpture for the Bijenkorf department store, Coolsingel, Rotterdam, 1954
right: Naum Gabo sculpture emphasising interiority of form.

Mutsuro Sasaki and Arata Isozaki, Train station competition scheme, Florence, 2002
far right: Rendering showing the organic quality of the structural system.

A structural design paradigm shift in architecture is enhancing a holistic building tectonic in which structure operates as a generator of form. At once intricate and fundamental, subtle and dramatic, structure now demands a deep and rigorous theory beyond that of methods of standard engineering practice.[1] Unlike buildings with skins that are mediatic display surfaces, a new structural synthesis combines bones and skin similar to an integrated industrial design object. A structurally led design theory can complete the trajectory from Pugin, with the interest in constructing decoration, to Ruskin, with the interest in decorating construction, and back again to a holistic integration of structure. Two emerging structural design strategies – 'deep decoration'[2] and 'subtle innovation' – provoke a complex, structurally based theory that returns structural design to a cultural and technological holism.

In defining a 21st-century structural theory, the engineer's work can no longer be taken for granted as a neutral speciality in technical prowess that responds to an architect's formal inquiry or material investigations, but is a creative endeavour in its own right. Engineers in the mid-20th century, such as the Spaniard Eduardo Torroja, understood this as more than a method of practice and emphasised: 'The process of visualizing or conceiving a structure is an art … motivated by an inner experience, by an intuition. It is never the result of mere deductive logical reasoning.'[3]

This definition of structural creativity is ever more evident in today's culture of technology where non-Cartesian, non-hierarchical and asymmetrical forms require an expanded structural syntax, both spatial and performative, for these increasingly integrated, complex projects involving collaborations between engineers and architects. For example, structural typologies can be categorised in a new lexicon from continuous floor-plate circulation, exoskeletons or long-span morphed structures in asymmetrically skewed space-frames. Complex topologies of non-linear, biomimetic forms are expressed in the work of engineer Mutsuro Sasaki and architect Arata Isozaki's Florence train station competition scheme (2009). Structural systems derived from algorithms, fractals or natural structures are then combined with intuition and experience. Such design shapes the future of complex and nonlinear space.

Since the work of D'Arcy Thompson,[4] the complexity of natural structures has specifically captured the interest of engineers and, in a deeper understanding of the relationships of elements to a whole in such instances as soap bubbles, coral, bone, crystals, beehives or sponges, blurred the distinction between the structure and the thing itself. One usually thinks of structure as opening up space, but an expansive scientific complexity is manifested in an understanding of filling space with structure that is occupiable. In the 1920s, architect Hermann Finsterlin discussed the interiority of organic nature – as organic form lies between crystalline and the amorphous, growing out of one another. The holism visible through scientific analysis in biological and natural structures parallels an interest in architectural structure and form. In the 1950s Kathleen Lonsdale, a crystallographer, identified the pattern of the solidity of the atom as a regularity of the internal structure and developed X-rays to photograph the depth of the crystals, noting that 'they have beauty in themselves and they can be obtained in infinite variety because the number and kinds of crystals is unlimited'.[5]

At the same time, scientist Lancelot White proposed that culture was shifting from the 'simple towards the complex, with the result that a modern conception of structure is, for some purposes, replacing the older conceptions of atomism and of form'. In this new relationship of parts to whole he envisioned that a 'unifying natural philosophy of the coming period may be a morphology, a doctrine of form viewed as structure'.[6] The relationship of parts to whole was also explicit in the Constructivist sculptures of the 1960s by Max Bill, Naum Gabo, Yenceslav Richter and Erwin Hauer, in which voids and volumes are interchangeable such that the interiority is filled with a spatial articulation of structural elements and space flows along a structure of sculpture, doubling as surface.[7]

Deep Decoration
Renewed investigations into the structure of natural life encourage cross-disciplinary collaborations leading to typologies in which structure is both subtle and emphatic, and seen in the resulting deep decoration as a holistic spatial structure. The integration of structural elements that function and provide a decoration thus creates a complex space. In Gestalt psychology, perception is understood as having laws of proximity, grouping and closure, demonstrating that patterns have an innate appeal because of the visual continuity and relationship between things, where the knowledge of the pattern plays out continuously as

Guy Nordenson and
Michael Maltzan, Jet
Propulsion Laboratory,
Pasadena, California, 2009
opposite: Interiority of the
structural system.

below: Project
development scheme
for structure showing
the gridded moment
frame.

bottom: Exterior
rendering.

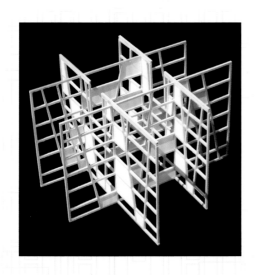

Subtle innovation combined with deep decoration creates a new holism in such projects as the Jet Propulsion Laboratory under construction in Pasadena, California, by architect Michael Maltzan with engineer Guy Nordenson.

SPAN Architects
(Matias del Campo and
Sandra Manninger) and
Arkan Zeytinoglu with
Jeroen Coenders (Arup),
Austrian Pavilion,
Shanghai Expo 2010
below: Arup construction
sequence diagrams.

right: Axonometric
showing the
layering of structure
and space.

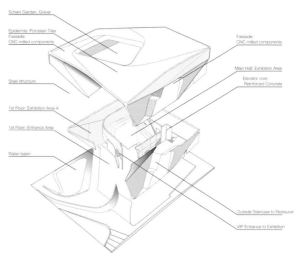

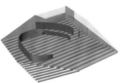

1 ground floor structure

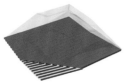

2 concrete walls

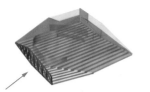

3 cantilevering truss

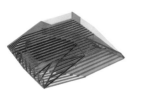

4 steel tripod

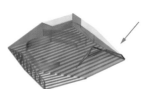

5 first floor structure

6 castellated beam
and spine

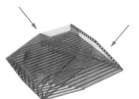

7 roof structure

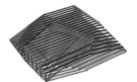

8 skin

a satisfying visual array. Deep decoration therefore results from integrating structure as part of a project where the parts to the whole have a meaningful and necessary relationship.

One such example is *The Dawn Line* (2009), part of the 'The Morning Line' series by artist Matthew Ritchie. A potentially inhabitable sculpture, it is both solid and void. Mathew Ritchie, working with Daniel Bosia of the Advanced Geometry Unit (AGU) at Arup London and architects Benjamin Aranda and Chris Lasch who are fascinated with crystals, here repeated algorithms of fractal geometries, propagating self-similar structural, tetrahedron three-dimensional cells. The 'bits', as they call them, can change in scale and carry the weight of the aluminium alloy structural assemblage. Here, it is the organisational principles – one seeking to integrate structure through the unity of surface ornamentation, and the other seeking to maintain a structural holism – that create deep decoration.

A deep decoration structural syntax is also evident in the current work of Reiser + Umemoto, such as their O-14 Tower in Dubai (2010) designed with engineer Ysrael A Seinuk. The 22-storey building has a structural skin that is holistic as performative decoration. Over a thousand apertures, whose size and orientation is determined by the sun angles and views, puncture a 40-centimetre (15.7-inch) thick concrete shell resulting in an expressive relationship to the structure.

The structural composition of Jürgen Mayer H's Metropol Parasol marketplace and cultural centre in Seville (2010), designed with engineer Volker Schmid from Arup, played a large part in the project's ultimate design. For the initial competition scheme, the building's skin contained an empty volume. As Schmid developed the project, a gridded structured volume in timber, cut like a topiary tree within the parasol, enabled the asymmetrical shape. The volume's north–south rectangular grid was thus juxtaposed with the organic outline of the parasol, resulting in both curves and linearity in a sculptural design similar to cutting through a tree trunk to reveal the rings. The deep decoration results in a holism of interiority as it relates to the expressive form.

Subtle Innovation

Other methods of design have also informed structures in terms of the integration of subtle innovations – small structural

A continuous ramp leads towards the recessed entrance of the building, creating a seamless connection between interior and exterior.

manoeuvres that impact the architectural design of a project in a larger way. Peter Rice's inventive glass curtain-walls with their spider-like clips for projects such as the Pyramid at the Louvre by IM Pei (1985), allow the glass to appear to be floating in weightless suspense. The structural facade of Beinecke Rare Book and Manuscript Library (1959) at Yale University, designed by Gordon Bunschaft of Skidmore, Owings & Merrill with engineers Paul Weidlinger and Matthys Levy, is a far-reaching experimental design. The grid of steel columns and beams acts as a girder, or multistorey Vierendeel truss, which spans to the four edges of the rectilinear building with the columns inset from the corners, organising the building design as a cohesive object. An invention of the engineers, rather than the building's architect, its weight is offset by a luminous stone and structural subtlety.

Subtle innovation combined with deep decoration creates a new holism in such projects as the Jet Propulsion Laboratory under construction in Pasadena, California, by architect Michael Maltzan with engineer Guy Nordenson. For the design of the planned 8,918-square-metre (96,000-square-foot) administration building, they were asked to make a flexible and collaborative interior workspace in a highly seismic zone. Nordenson, working with engineers Simpson Gumpertz & Heger, conceived of a distributed core structure rather than a traditional monolithic central core. This point of innovation formed a dynamic, interconnected structure, reflecting and fostering the institution's inventive spirit.

The lateral-resisting structure is organised along four vertical diaphragms that extend north and south, dividing each floor plate in three, and in three again, forming a nine-square grid that scatters the building core's vertical shafts to form a series of double-height collaboration spaces, like a three-dimensional tick-tack-toe. The four frames are a combination of moment frames and break frames and visibly transverse the building, functioning to resist the seismic forces. Diagonal braces stiffen the structure, and are positioned to maintain the open circulation. The diagonals are scattered in a confetti-like quality populating the four planes and are visible in the elevation, informing the facade and the patterning of the square apertures and also creating the deep decoration. The facade is thus integrated with the structure as a tessellation, reflecting both inwards and outwards the complex structural interiority of the project.

Holistic and fluid buildings push the limits of space-making guided by the geometries responsible for Gottfried Semper's knot, the Klein bottle, and the Möbius strip, as well as non-linear space as defined by Gilles Deleuze or Manuel De Landa. For example, non-linear forms can result from a 'smooth' Deleuzian space between the structure and the space itself, singularising it as a radical modelling. Holism provides a meaningful paradigm wherein interiority is a synthesis of structural elements.

SPAN Architects' design, with Arkan Zeytinoglu of Zeytinoglu ZT GmbH, for the Austrian Pavilion for the Shanghai Expo 2010, was a collaboration with engineer Jeroen Coenders of Arup Amsterdam that resulted in a holistic volume based on efficiency in the nature of topological organisation. Four structural elements – a tripod framework, cantilevered truss, castellated beam and a main box-girder spine in the middle – allow for the opening of a continuous volume that loops around a central courtyard. The topological organisation mimics the efficiency of natural structures such as bones, being expressive, fluid and connected. The building becomes at once formal, performative, hybrid, decorative and structural.

In the synthesis of structure and form, structure as deep decoration combined with subtle innovation has evolved from a new culture of technology and design, shaping complex space and resulting in a structurally led design theory. This new structural theory reveals a space that parallels the understanding of the complexity of natural structures, leading to an even more expansive potential for a new structural paradigm and design aesthetic. ◬

Notes
1. The basis for a 'good' structural practice since Eiffel has been that of efficiency, economy and beauty. While significant as a set of principles, this is not a theory of structure but a method of practice.
2. Nina Rappaport, 'Deep Decoration', *306090*, Princeton Architecture Press (New York), Fall 2006, was the first publication to define this concept.
3. Eduardo Torroja, *Philosophy of Structures*, trans JJ Polivka and Milos Polivka, University of California Press (Berkeley, CA), 1958, p 313.
4. The early 20th-century biologist and zoologist D'Arcy Thompson is a continued reference by both historical and contemporary designers and engineers for his detailed descriptions of animal structures in his 1919 book, *On Growth and Form*.
5. Kathleen Lonsdale, 'Crystal structure', in Gyorgy Kepes (ed), *Structure in Art and Science*, George Braziller (New York), 1954, pp 358–9.
6. Lancelot White, 'Atomism, structure, and form', in Kepes op cit, pp 20–2.
7. George Rickey, *Constructivism, Origins and Evolution*, George Braziller (New York), 1967.

Text © 2010 John Wiley & Sons Ltd. Images: pp 122-3 © Jürgen Mayer H Architects; p 124(l) © Matthew Ritchie, photo Stephen Brayne; p 124(r) © Imre Solt; p 125(l) © Nina Rappaport; p 125(r) © Arata Isozaki & Associates; pp 126-7 © Michael Maltzan Architects, Inc; pp 128-9 © SPAN 2010, photo Alfred Roider

COUNTERPOINT
04/2010
Nº 206
AD

DIGITAL SOLIPSISM AND THE PARADOX OF THE GREAT 'FORGETTING'

Neil Spiller counters the main theme of this issue by questioning the dominant focus on production and new technologies in architectural culture, which places a premium on the generation of 'ever more gratuitous complex surfaces and structures'. Could this inward-looking emphasis on process and obsessive love of new technologies be at the expense of the final product? Are we in danger of producing artefacts that lose sight of human expression and poetics in the competitive drive for greater complexity? Are we, in fact, heading towards a great 'forgetting' in which humanity is subtracted from the architectural product?

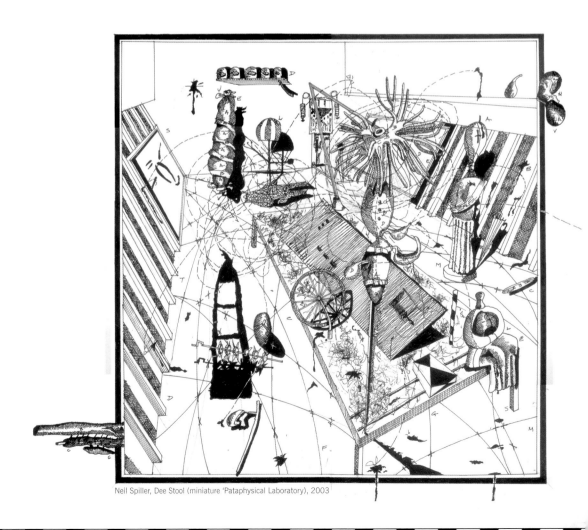

Neil Spiller, Dee Stool (miniature 'Pataphysical Laboratory), 2003

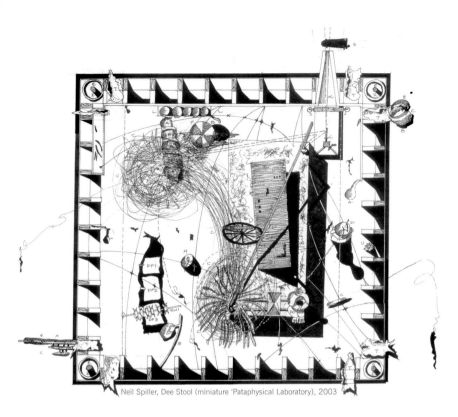

Neil Spiller, Dee Stool (miniature 'Pataphysical Laboratory'), 2003

Architecture has numerous nuances that late Modernism has forgotten. Enigma, memory, mythology and quotational poetics are crucial to the prospect of creating architectures that invigorate all aspects of the human mind and not just the human pocket. The continued reductivism of architectural discourse into the computability of surfaces and double-curved forms belies an inability of the architectural profession to fully engage the complex articulations that architecture must evolve in order to contribute to social and political critical debates.

The Idea of Truth is the most imaginary of solutions.
Christian Bok, *'Pataphysics: The Poetics of an Imaginary Science*, 2002, p 18[1]

Neither a fine art or a science, architecture has only recently begun to realize its true potential, mainly through a hermeneutic approach that can engage the intricacies of its historical reality. Yet teaching and practice continue to be polarized between those two false alternatives: fine art and applied science.
The introduction of computers into architecture during the last two decades has helped reduce architectural discourse to issues of instrumentality. The most popular discussions presume the importance of this so-called paradigm shift and focus on the potential and limitations of this instrument, aiding the perpetuation of the dichotomy. Thus theoretical discourse tends to remain caught up in instrumental issues of form (innovation) and production (efficiency), while the humanistic dimension of architecture is further jeopardised and educational programs become increasingly vocational.
Alberto Pérez-Gómez, *Built Upon Love: Architectural Longing after Ethics and Aesthetics*, 2008, p 199[2]

This edition of Δ can be applauded for its attempt to theorise the 'new' processes and techniques of making and fabricating building and the emerging opportunities in the convergence of engineering and architecture. However, it is important to demand for architecture an approach to architectural production which, while valuing the new hybrid notions of making, also predicates its output on poetics. Much recent architecture, especially the well-known examples, has been devoid of humanity and panders to a need for ever more gratuitous complex surfaces and structures. This justifies or obscures their simple, apolitical and vacuous objectives. Our short-sightedness caused by the development of ever more dexterous 'printing' technology, the ubiquity of global capitalism and the myth of the deity architect has encouraged a great 'forgetting' – a forgetting that has subtracted the humanity from the architectural products of our era. This forgetting is threatening to ruin good schools of architecture, their graduating students and the profession that they enter.

Architecture and its creation is a complex entity; it cannot all be wholly produced by computers – no matter how powerful or how artificially intelligent they may be. Architects need to be taught to understand the intricacies of space and the various yardsticks that can be used to measure it – and equally the number of creative tactics that can be used to create it. I'm not arguing here for

some Luddite future, but for a symbiotic use of new technology with an understanding of the human longing to express humanity's rich spectrum of aspirations and hopes in architecture and its lineaments. I'm also not arguing here for a resurgent historically based Postmodernism style in architecture. I am arguing for an architecture that is not just about itself, that is not just narcissistic. An architecture that engages with humanity, its joys and fears, its actual and mnemonic context and its aspirations towards cross-cultural citizenry. This is hard to do, as Alberto Perez-Gomez states:

> Poetic forms such as architecture seek participation by speaking not about the speaker but about the 'world' by expressing not technologic control or political domination but true wonder and the supreme mystery of humankind … the difficulty of such a task should not be underestimated, however. Contemporary mental pathologies notwithstanding, modern man and woman remain determined to exclude whatever cannot be articulated through logical reason.[3]

The Royalty of Science and the Nomadity of Architecture

In our era we are led to believe that the pursuit of scientific knowledge is predicated on precedent, just like the law. Science

131

Lebbeus Woods, Epicylarium, 1984–5

Scientific concepts are refined over
time with an epistemology that
is about honing, simplifying, and
reducing down to a fundamental,
inescapable, holistic truth.

allegedly utilises controlled experiment
through clear, succinct methodology and
specific unambiguous language. Scientific
concepts are refined over time with
an epistemology that is about honing,
simplifying, and reducing down to a
fundamental, inescapable, holistic truth.
Further, this truth has become consistent and
accepted across the universe, at all scales
(from the microcosmic to the macrocosmic)
and in all matter, organic and inorganic.
Any worldview short of this ideological
dictatorship is pushed into the realm of 'art',
a world populated by erratic sophists – a
world ultimately useless and marginalised.
It is through this meta-methodology that
science holds and controls society's reins.
Without this form of empirical tyranny, other
approaches might not be so easily dismissed
as arcane or even evilly occult. Christian Bok
describes this condition as 'what Deleuze
and Guattari might call the royal sciences of
efficient productivity [which] have historically
repressed and exploited the nomad sciences
of expedient adaptability'.[4]

At their root, the royal sciences seem to
have a misconception about language and
communication. Language has a propensity
for inaccuracy, for personalisation, for
misconstruing and misreading meaning,
for relativity. It is also emotively subjective.
Scientists perceive themselves as fighting
against this ontology of language and
asking us to believe in their (own) objective
and ubiquitous language to describe their

allegedly ubiquitous knowledge. It is here that
science's biggest error has been made, and
it is here that poetry through its acceptance
of the ontology of language can offer a more
fecund way of seeing the world.

Architects must not be radical solipsists,
believing that everything in the world is
dependent on their perception of it. One might
consider the model of the second-order
cyberneticist and that of radical Constructivists.
The conversation between an architect's work
and the user/viewer of it should be able to
evolve in all manner of different ways, some
of which will have been considered by me
and others not. In short, it is reflexive and
often beyond full creative control. It is full of
elision and illusion, feedback and
readjustment, dependent on the system and
its observers. Further, the radical
Constructivist acknowledges that we make
our worlds by interacting with them and that
they are all different, exceptional, particular.

'Pataphysics and Exceptions

While a second-order cybernetic
understanding of our worlds is useful, we
should also consider design conversations
that use the errant poetics of Alfred Jarry's
'pataphysics (apostrophe deliberate). It
is my opinion that the two paradigms are
not mutually exclusive as both deal in the
particular and the exceptional.

Along with the creation of Père Ubu,
Jarry is remembered for his creation of Doctor
Faustroll and the 'science' of 'pataphysics:

Lebbeus Woods, Einstein Tomb – Perspective from Space, 1984–5

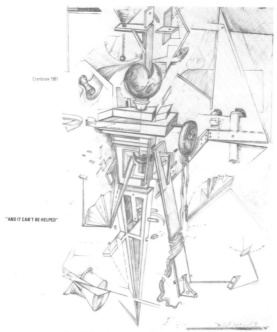

Daniel Libeskind, And it Can't be Helped, 1981

Daniel Libeskind, 11 The Other Side: Ikon and Idea, 1978

'Pataphysics had appeared in Jarry's most early work, but in 1898 he wrote the *Exploits and Opinions of Doctor Faustroll, Pataphysician* (not published until 1911). This book set out the sketchy outlines of the poetic affrontery that is 'pataphysics. 'Pataphysics is the science of the realm beyond metaphysics … It will study the laws which govern exceptions and will explain the universe supplementary to this one; or less ambitiously it will describe a universe which one can see – must see perhaps – instead of the traditional one … Definition: 'Pataphysics is the science of imaginary solutions, which symbolically attributes the properties of objects, described by their virtuality, to their lineaments.'[5]

All of Jarry's prose and poetics are predicated on what Christian Bok has called the 'Three Declensions of 'Pataphysics'. These are the algorithm of Jarry's art: Anamalos (the principle of Variance), Syzygia (the Principle of Alliance) and Clinamen (the Principle of Deviance). Jarry named the ability of a system to swerve, the Clinamen, in reference to Lucretius's poem *De rerum natura* (the minimal swerve of an atom).

In *Subliminal Note* (1960), Roger Shattuck attempts to define 'pataphysics, a task he calls 'self-contradictory':

'Pataphysics relates each thing and each event not to any generality (a mere plastering over of exceptions) but to a

singularity that makes it an exception. … In the realm of the particular, every event arises from an infinite number of causes … Students of philosophy may remember the German Hans Vaihinger with his philosophy of als ob. Ponderously yet persistently he declared that we construct our own system of thought and value, and then live 'as if' reality conformed to it.[6]

The importance of both 'pataphysics and the radical Constructivism of some second-order cyberneticists has a common philosophical precedent. The notion that by being in, observing and operating in the world we construct personal epistemologies is a trait of both paradigms. It is a way of thinking that is connected to the world and yet beyond it, which is a precedent an architecture would benefit from remembering. Bok writes: 'As to understand on behalf of truth is to be reactive, accepting the world of the "as is", but to misunderstand on behalf of error is to be creative, inventing the world of the as if'.[7]

The Vision
Where does all this lead? It leads to a vision for contemporary architecture, a vision that is probably just out of reach right now but soon will be attainable. It is an architecture that dovetails into its site at not just the anthropocentric scale but at ecological scales, microcosmic and cosmoscopic scales. An architecture that has the capacity to reboot torn ecologies with helpful architectonic scaffolds, which dismantle themselves

when all is well again. An architecture that traps more carbon than its environmental footprint. An architecture that contributes to the health of its users and its environment. An architecture that hasn't forgotten history, poetics or how we are all different. An architecture that rejoices in that difference. An architecture whose exquisite tailoring is imbued with nuances that resonate with familiar and non-familiar 'worlds'. An architecture that knows where it is and why it is and what it has to offer, but doesn't deny its difference and ours.

This surely must be any architect's personal goal in the 21st century – a goal that denies ill-fitted containers and the design of objects as obstacles. Architecture that digitally, historically, uncannily and ecologically doesn't FORGET. An architecture led by structural expedience seldom delivers the rich tapestry of multivalent parameters so desperately needed in today's fast-moving world. ⌂

Notes
1. C Bok, *'Pataphysics: The Poetics of an Imaginary Science*, North Western Press (Illinois), 2002, p 18.
2. Alberto Pérez-Gómez, *Built Upon Love: Architectural Longing after Ethics and Aesthetics*, MIT Press (Cambridge, MA), 2008, p 199.
3. Pérez-Gómez, op cit, p 198.
4. Bok, op cit, p 14.
5. Alfred Jarry, *Exploits and Opinions of Doctor Faustroll, 'Pataphysician: A Scientific Novel*, trans Simon Watson Taylor, Grove Press (London), 1965, p 6.
6. R Shattuck, 'Subliminal Note', *Evergreen Review*, Vol 4, No 13, 1960.
7. Bok, op cit, p 18.

Text © 2010 John Wiley & Sons Ltd. Images: pp 130-1 © Neil Spiller; pp 132-3 © Lebbeus Woods; pp 134-5 © Studio Daniel Libeskind

Frank Barkow has been a partner, with Regine Leibinger, of Barkow Leibinger Architects, Berlin, since 1993. He studied architecture at Montana State University and at Harvard's Graduate School of Design. He has taught at the Architectural Association (AA) in London, Cornell University and at Harvard.

Martin Bechthold is Professor of Architectural Technology, Director of the Fabrication Labs, and Co-director of the Master in Design Studies Program at the Harvard Graduate School of Design. His teaching and research focus on structural systems and lightweight structures, parametric design and digital fabrication methods, and robotic fabrication methods. His work studies emerging technologies that allow for new opportunities in the design and making of architectural constructs. He is author of *Innovative Surface Structures: Technologies and Applications* (Taylor & Francis, 2007), *Digital Design and Manufacturing: CAD/CAM Applications in Architecture and Design* (John Wiley & Sons, 2005) and *Structures* (Prentice Hall, 2007).

Klaus Bollinger and Manfred Grohmann established their practice Bollinger + Grohmann in Darmstadt in 1983, and are today located in Frankfurt am Main, Vienna and Paris. The internationally operating consulting engineers are collaborating with a large variety of architects including Coop Himmelb(l)au, SANAA, Dominique Perrault, Zaha Hadid, Peter Cook, Frank Gehry, Hans Hollein, Toyo Ito, Claude Vasconi and Christoph Mäckler. Both engineers also teach at architectural faculties: Klaus Bollinger at the University for Applied Arts in Vienna and Manfred Grohmann at Kassel University. Oliver Tessmann is working for Bollinger + Grohmann at the interface of architecture and engineering after receiving his doctoral degree in 2008.

Julio Martínez Calzón is a structural engineer and President of the MC2 Engineering consultancy office in Madrid. With more than 40 years' experience in designing bridges and special structures, he has collaborated with many world-renowned architects such as Norman Foster, Santiago Calatrava, Rafael Moneo, Ieoh Ming Pei, Juan Navarro Baldeweg, Tadao Ando, Arata Isozaki and others. Some of his most outstanding works include the Palau Sant Jordi (Isozaki), Collserola Tower (Foster), Canal Theaters (Navarro Baldeweg) and Torre Espacio (Pei, Cobb, Freed and partners). With Miralles Tagliabue EMBT he has collaborated very closely in several projects, such as the Gas Natural Office Building and the Spanish Pavilion for the 2010 Expo in Shanghai, and is currently working with the practice on several other projects. Carlos Castañón Jiménez is a structural engineer and Director of the MC2 Engineering office. He has worked with Martínez Calzón for the past eight years, collaborating on several bridges and special building projects. He has been the engineer in charge of the structural design and analysis for the Spanish Pavilion, and is currently collaborating with EMBT on several other projects.

John Chilton is Professor of Architecture and Design at the School of Architecture Design and Built Environment, Nottingham Trent University. He has written widely about the work of Heinz Isler and his own research interests in the field of non-conventional structures. He is an active member of the International Association for Shell and Spatial Structures (IASS) in Madrid.

Fabio Gramazio and Matthias Kohler are professors for Architecture and Digital Fabrication at the ETH Zurich. They are joint partners in the architects' office Gramazio + Kohler in Zurich. Their work has been awarded numerous prizes and is exhibited internationally. It includes a single-family home in Riedikon, the Christmas illuminations in the Zurich Bahnhofstrasse as well as the contemporary dance institution Tanzhaus Zurich. With their research facility at ETH Zurich they contributed the exhibition design 'Structural Oscillations' for the Swiss Pavilion at the 11th Venice Biennale. In 2008 they published *Digital Materiality in Architecture*. Before their appointment as professors, Kohler was faculty at the Professorships Marc Angelil and Greg Lynn at ETH Zurich, and Gramazio worked for the Professorship of Architecture and CAAD. Gramazio is also a co-founder of the etoy art project. Silvan Oesterle is an architect based in Zurich and faculty at the Professorship for Architecture and Digital Fabrication (ETH Zurich). He is the co-founder of ROK, a design and research agency exploring the relationships between architecture, manufacturing and computation. He has given lectures at various schools, conferences and offices among which are the AA in London, the ULC ESARQ School of Architecture (Barcelona), the Smart Geometry Conference (Munich) and UNStudio (Amsterdam). In 2007 he earned a Master of Science in Architecture from ETH Zurich. He has worked as a designer for UNStudio and Riarch (New York).

Dominik Holzer set up the international think tank AEC Connect for developing strategies to connect the architecture, engineering and construction industries. He now works with BVN Architecture across Australia after finishing his PhD on sense-making in transdisciplinary design at the Spatial Information Architecture Laboratory (SIAL) at the Royal Melbourne Institute of Technology (RMIT). During his PhD research, he was embedded at Arup in Melbourne and Sydney where he collaborated closely with Steven Downing, an IT/engineering support specialist whose role at Arup is to help realise complex structures through scripting, parametric design and computation. Both authors have commented on the cultural context of architectural and engineering design computation in various publications and are closely affiliated with the SmartGeometry group.

Hanif Kara is a structural engineer and co-founder of Adams Kara Taylor (AKT), the design-led structural and civil engineering consultancy based in London. As design director, he has worked on award-winning projects throughout Europe. He is currently a visiting professor of Architectural Technology at Kungliga Tekniska Högskolan (KTH) Stockholm, and is the Pierce Anderson visiting critic for Creative Engineering at Harvard's Graduate School of Design. He was selected for the master jury for the 2004 cycle of the Aga Khan Awards for Architecture. He is the first structural engineer to be appointed a commissioner at the Commission for Architecture and the Built Environment (CABE) where he co-chairs the design review panel and chairs the Inclusive Design Group. He is a Fellow of the Institution of Structural Engineers, an Honorary Fellow of the Royal Institute of British Architects (RIBA) and a Fellow of the Royal Society of Arts.

Wolf Mangelsdorf studied architecture and civil engineering at Karlsruhe University, where he also worked for an architectural practice after graduation. After a research stay at Kyoto University he moved to the UK in 1997 to work as a structural engineer at Anthony Hunt Associates in its Cirencester and London offices. Since 2002 he has been with Buro Happold in London where he is now a partner, responsible for structural engineering in the London office, and project principal for a wide range of multidisciplinary projects all over the world. His large portfolio of current projects includes the redevelopment of Battersea Power Station, the Museum of Transport in Glasgow, Cairo Expo City and Médiacité Liège. He has been teaching technical studies at the AA Diploma School since 2000 and has been a guest lecturer and guest tutor at a number of universities internationally.

Neri Oxman is an architect and researcher whose work establishes a new approach to design at the interface of computer science, material engineering and ecology. She is the founder of an interdisciplinary design initiative, MATERIALECOLOGY, and has recently completed her PhD at MIT as a presidential fellow. Her *Natural Artifice* work has recently been displayed in the Museum of Modern Art's 'Design and the Elastic Mind' exhibition, and is now part of the museum's collection. She has won multiple awards for her research including the HOLCIM Next Generation Award for Sustainable Construction, a Graham Foundation Carter Manny Award, the AICF Award of Excellence, the Harold Horowitz Award, the International Earth Award for Future-Crucial Design, and a METROPOLIS Next Generation Award. She has taught, lectured and published widely. In September 2010, she is due to establish a new research group at MIT's Media Lab based on her work and research in design computation.

Helmut Pottmann received a PhD in mathematics from Vienna University of Technology (TU Wien) in 1983. Since 1992 he has been a professor at TU Wien and Head of the Geometric Modelling and Industrial Geometry research group. His recent research concentrates on geometric computing for architecture and manufacturing.

Nina Rappaport is an architectural critic, curator and educator. She is Publications Director at Yale School of Architecture, and editor of the biannual publication *Constructs*, the exhibition catalogues, and the school's book series. Her current research projects focus on the intersection of urban design and infrastructure, innovative engineering and places of production, and she is currently working on an exhibition on the 'Vertical Urban Factory'. She is the author of *Support and Resist: Structural Engineers and Design Innovation* (Monacelli Press, 2007) and co-author of *Long Island City: Connecting the Arts* (Episode Books, 2006), and has contributed essays to numerous books and journals. She currently teaches in the Syracuse (New York City) programme and has taught studios and seminars on the post-industrial factory, urbanism and innovative engineers at Barnard/Columbia College, City College, Parsons School of Design and Yale School of Architecture.

Fabian Scheurer is a founding partner of designtoproduction and leads the company's office in Zurich. After graduating from the Technical University of Munich with a degree in computer science and architecture, he worked as an assistant for the university's CAAD group, as software developer for CAD provider Nemetschek, and as a new media consultant for Eclat AG in Zurich. From 2002 until 2006 he studied the use of artificial-life methods in architectural construction as a member of Ludger Hovestadt's CAAD group at the ETH Zurich, and managed to transfer the results to a number of collaborative projects between architects, engineers and fabrication experts. In 2005 he co-founded designtoproduction as a research group to explore the connections between digital design and fabrication. At the end of 2006 designtoproduction teamed up with architect Arnold Walz and became a commercial consulting practice, since then having implemented digital production chains for projects like Zaha Hadid's Hungerburg funicular in Innsbruck, the EPFL Learning Center in Lausanne (SANAA), and the Centre Pompidou in Metz (Shigeru Ban). He is a visiting professor at the AA School's EmTech programme in London.

Werner Sobek was educated as both an architect and a structural engineer, and has been a full-time professor at the University of Stuttgart since 1995. He has also taught as Mies van der Rohe Professor at the IIT in Chicago since 2008. While his university role specialises in research into new materials and new concepts for lightweight and adaptive structures, Werner Sobek's office is one of the world's leading consultancies for engineering, design and green technologies. The office was founded in 1992 and now has branches in Stuttgart, Cairo, Dubai, Frankfurt, Moscow and New York.

Neil Spiller is Professor of Architecture and Digital Theory and a practising architect. He is the Graduate Director of Design, Director of the Advanced Virtual and Technological Architecture Research Group (AVATAR) and Vice Dean at the Bartlett School of Architecture, UCL. His books include *Visionary Architecture: Blueprints of the Modern Imagination* (Thames & Hudson, 2006) and *Digital Architecture NOW* (Thames & Hudson, 2008), a compendium of contemporary digital architectural practice.

Yves Weinand is an architect and structural engineer, and founder of the Bureau d'Etudes Weinand in Liège. He is currently working on the ice rink in Liège and the parliament building in Lausanne, where timber is used as the structural component. Since 2004 he has been Professor and Head of the IBOIS laboratory for timber constructions at the École Polytechnique Fédérale de Lausanne (EPFL). Here he directs an interdisciplinary group of architects, engineers, mathematicians and computer scientists who perform research work in the fields of timber rib shells, folded timber plate structures and woven timber structures. Markus Hudert studied architecture at the University of Applied Sciences in Coburg and completed his postgraduate studies in conceptual design at the Städelschule in Frankfurt in 2002. From 2003 to 2006 he was based in the Netherlands, where he worked for UNStudio and Benthem Crouwel Architects. Since 2006 he has been research and teaching assistant at IBOIS where he is currently working on his doctoral thesis.

INDIVIDUAL BACKLIST ISSUES OF △D ARE AVAILABLE FOR PURCHASE AT £22.99/US$45. TO ORDER AND SUBSCRIBE SEE BELOW

What is Architectural Design?

Founded in 1930, *Architectural Design* (△D) is an influential and prestigious publication. It combines the currency and topicality of a newsstand journal with the rigour and production qualities of a book. With an almost unrivalled reputation worldwide, it is consistently at the forefront of cultural thought and design.

Each title of △D is edited by an invited guest-editor, who is an international expert in the field. Renowned for being at the leading edge of design and new technologies, △D also covers themes as diverse as: architectural history, the environment, interior design, landscape architecture and urban design.

Provocative and inspirational, △D inspires theoretical, creative and technological advances. It questions the outcome of technical innovations as well as the far-reaching social, cultural and environmental challenges that present themselves today.

Purchasing Architectural Design

Individual titles of △D are sold as books through specialist retailers and flagship bookstores and by online booksellers. It can also be purchased directly from Wiley at www.wiley.com. △D can be bought on annual subscription. Special rates are offered for students and individual professionals as well as to institutions.

How to Subscribe

With 6 issues a year, you can subscribe to △D (either print or online), or buy titles individually.

Subscribe today to receive 6 issues delivered direct to your door!

INSTITUTIONAL SUBSCRIPTION
£198 / US$369 combined
print & online

INSTITUTIONAL SUBSCRIPTION
£180 / US$335 print or online

PERSONAL RATE SUBSCRIPTION
£110 / US$170 print only

STUDENT RATE SUBSCRIPTION
£70 / US$110 print only

To subscribe:
Tel: +44 (0) 843 828
Email: cs-journals@wiley.com

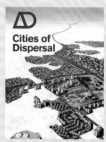

Volume 78 No 1
ISBN 978 0470 066379

Volume 78 No 2
ISBN 978 0470 516874

Volume 78 No 3
ISBN 978 0470 512548

Volume 78 No 4
ISBN 978 0470 519479

Volume 78 No 5
ISBN 978 0470 751220

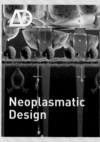

Volume 78 No 6
ISBN 978 0470 519585

Volume 79 No 1
ISBN 978 0470 997796

Volume 79 No 2
ISBN 978 0470 998205

Volume 79 No 3
ISBN 978 0470 753637

Volume 79 No 4
ISBN 978 0470 773000

Volume 79 No 5
ISBN 978 0470 699553

Volume 79 No 6
ISBN 978 0470 699591

Volume 80 No 1
ISBN 978 0470 743195

Volume 80 No 2
ISBN 978 0470 717141

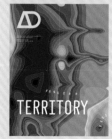

Volume 80 No 3
ISBN 978 0470 721650